Discover...

Topics for Advanced Learners
Series Editor: Klaus Hinz

English Newspapers and Television

Teachers' Book

By Stephen Speight and Anno Ortmeier

Best. Nr. 40063 0

Verlag Ferdinand Schöningh

Gedruckt auf umweltfreundlichem, chlorfrei gebleichtem Papier.

Alle deutschsprachigen Teile dieses Werks folgen der reformierten Rechtschreibung und Zeichensetzung.

Umschlagentwurf: Veronika Wypior

© 1999 Verlag Ferdinand Schöningh, Paderborn
(Verlag Ferdinand Schöningh, Jühenplatz 1, 33098 Paderborn)

Alle Rechte vorbehalten. Dieses Werk sowie einzelne Teile desselben sind urheberrechtlich geschützt. Jede Verwertung in anderen als den gesetzlich zugelassenen Fällen ist ohne vorherige schriftliche Zustimmung des Verlages nicht zulässig.

Printed in Germany. Gesamtherstellung: Ferdinand Schöningh, Paderborn.

Druck 5 4 3 2 1   Jahr 03 02 01 00 99

ISBN 3-506-40063-0

Inhaltsverzeichnis

	Discover ...: Zielsetzung und methodischer Ansatz	4

Teil I – Die didaktische Konzeption

Das Thema "English Newspapers" im Englischunterricht 6
Das Thema "English Television" im Englischunterricht 6
Textauswahl 6
Tabellarische Textübersicht 8
Integration des Heftes in größere thematische
Zusammenhänge 10
Anbindung an Ganzschriften 11
Weiterführende Literatur 11

Teil II – Das Schülerbuch im Unterricht

Chapter 1: Newspapers 14
Vorbemerkungen zum Kapitel 14
Start here 14
The facts about 15
The Dunblane massacre 17
A review article: Look back in anger 19
A sensational news story: Mud-Hut-Rat 21
A leading article: A princess, a funeral and
a nation's sadness 24
A comment: The history of chess ends here 29
A column: Manhunt 32
A factual report: Giant gates keep sea at bay 36
A sports report: Serene Chang serves the Lord 38
Additional Text: Advertisement 43

Chapter 2: Television 45
Vorbemerkungen zum Kapitel 45
Start here 46
What's on TV this evening? 48
Classic comedy: Fawlty Towers 50
A police series: The Bill 54
Satirical comedy: Yes, Prime Minister 61
Costume drama: Pride and Prejudice 66

Postscript: The Media – Watchdog or Rottweiler? 73

Teil III – Klausurbeispiele

Klausur 1: William Leith, 'They might be spitting in the
cannelloni. This is what happens!' 78
Klausur 2: John Cleese and Connie Booth,
A Touch of Class 81

Discover ...:
Zielsetzung und methodischer Ansatz

Die Themenheftreihe Discover ... richtet sich an Schülerinnen und Schüler der Sekundarstufe II und bereitet in Anlehnung an den Themenkatalog der Richtlinien Englisch landeskundliche oder allgemeine, Jugendliche interessierende Themen methodisch-didaktisch auf. Die Verfahrensweise lehnt sich an neuere lernpsychologische Erkenntnisse an. Das besondere Merkmal liegt in der Bearbeitung der Texte anhand von *pre-reading-*, *while-reading-* und *post-reading*-Aufgaben.

Pre-reading Aufgaben führen zum Text, Thema oder Problem hin. Forschungsergebnisse belegen, dass eine interessante Texteröffnung einen positiven Einfluss auf die Textbegegnung hat. Die *pre-reading* Aufgaben konkretisieren zudem besonders das Vorwissen und bauen Erwartungshaltungen auf. Spezifische *pre-reading* Aufgaben finden sich in Form von Bild/Text-Collagen auf der in ein Kapitel einführenden „Start here"-Seite.

Beim ersten fortlaufenden Lesen kommen unterschiedliche textverarbeitende Operationen ins Spiel. Da hierzu in der Regel nur begrenzte Zeit zur Verfügung steht, ist eine Hilfstätigkeit darin zu sehen, beim Lesen von Zeit zu Zeit innezuhalten, um auf das bereits Gelesene zurückzublicken. Durch das verlangsamte Lesetempo können intensivere Interaktionen zwischen Leser und Text stattfinden. Reflexions- und Verstehenshilfen finden sich in *Discover ...* in den *while-reading*-Aufgaben und Beobachtungsanleitungen in der Randspalte. Sie begleiten den Lesevorgang und dienen gleichsam als *navigational aid*. Mit ihrer Hilfe wird das Verständnis der Oberflächenstruktur des Textes sichergestellt. Diese methodische Neuheit wird durch ein besonderes Layout, durch die Unterteilung der Seite in eine Textspalte und eine die *while-reading*-Aufgaben enthaltende Randspalte ermöglicht. Die mit Pfeilen versehenen Aufgaben begleiten den Lesevorgang. Sie haben vorwärtsweisenden, rückverweisenden oder statarischen Charakter. Ein nach unten weisender Pfeil (∇) verknüpft die Aufgabe mit dem nachfolgenden Text als so genannte Beobachtungsanleitung. Eine mit einem nach innen gerichteten Pfeil (◁) versehene Aufgabe bezieht sich auf die betreffende Textstelle und ein nach oben weisender Pfeil (△) zeigt an, dass sich die Aufgabe auf den gerade gelesenen Textteil bezieht und man sich rückblickend Klarheit über das Textverständnis verschaffen soll.

Alternativ zum *guided reading* können die Aufgaben der Randspalte auch erst nach dem Lesen mündlich oder schriftlich beantwortet werden; ihnen kommt dann die Funktion der üblichen *comprehension questions* zur Überprüfung des Textverständnisses zu. In diesem Fall überlesen die Schüler während des ersten Durchgangs die Fragen und Aufgaben zunächst.

Die sich an den Text anschließenden *Activities* sind vertiefender Natur. Sie beziehen sich auf die kreative Textproduktion sowie auf die Interpretation im weitesten Sinn. Damit wird auch der textanalytische Zugriff geschult.

Die Kombination von *pre-reading-*, *while-reading-* und *after-assignments* (*acivities*) ermöglicht eine an neuesten lernpsychologischen und methodischen Erkenntnissen orientierte Textbearbeitung im Sinne einer vermittelnden Methode, bei der Leser und Text gleichermaßen den ihnen zukommenden Stellenwert erhalten.

Teil I

Discover ... English Newspapers and Television:
Die didaktische Konzeption

Die didaktische Konzeption

Das Thema „English Newspapers" im Englischunterricht

Die Auseinandersetzung mit der britischen Presselandschaft zählt zu den zentralen Themen des Englischunterrichts in der Sek. II. Das erste Kapitel erarbeitet daher im Sinne einer ersten Orientierung zentrale Aspekte der breiten Palette der britischen Tagespresse, auf deren Kenntnis Teile der weiteren Textarbeit in der Oberstufe aufbauen. In diesen Kontext gehören die Differenzierung der Presselandschaft in *tabloid papers* und *serious papers* ebenso wie die unterschiedliche und häufig deutlich markierte politische Tendenz dieser Blätter, der für die einzelne Zeitung häufig charakteristische Umgang mit Text und Bild mit der entsprechenden Gewichtung dieser beiden Elemente, ihre genau definierte Zielgruppe sowie die Rolle der Presse im britischen Alltag. Das Schülerbuch will damit vor allem wesentliche Informationsquelle sein, wenn es darum geht, in einem Grund- oder Leistungskurs Wissen über unterschiedliche Textformate aus dem Bereich der schriftlichen Medien zu erarbeiten, es trägt zur methodischen wie inhaltlichen Schulung in Rezeption wie Produktion solcher Texte bei und hilft beim Aufbau eines metasprachlichen Wortschatzes zu diesem Sachbereich.

Das Thema „English Television" im Englischunterricht

Das Fernsehen ist wie die Presse ein wichtiges Informations- und Unterhaltungsmedium. Es ist daher ein wichtiges Ziel des Unterrichts, Schülerinnen und Schüler mit den Besonderheiten des englischen Fernsehens bekannt zu machen. Das zweite Kapitel dieses Buches bietet dazu ausgewähltes Material. Video und Fernsehen haben schon lange ihren Platz im Englischunterricht der Sekundarstufe II gefunden und methodisch-didaktische Überlegungen, die sich auch in Richtlinien niederschlagen, betonen mehr und mehr ihren Wert. Es gilt, das Medium als Arbeitsgrundlage mit einer breiten Palette sinnvoller und motivierender Arbeits- und Aufgabenformen im Englischunterricht zu etablieren. Einen Beitrag dazu kann das vorliegende Arbeitsmaterial leisten, wenn auch die Videobänder eingesetzt werden.

Textauswahl

Die Materialien der beiden Hauptkapitel wurden nach jeweils unterschiedlichen Kriterien ausgewählt. Für das Kapitel *Newspapers* ist der Versuch unternommen worden, die gebräuchlichsten Textformate journalistischer Arbeit einzubeziehen. Im Wesentlichen handelt es sich dabei um *comment, news story, leading article, sports report*. Jedem Textsortenbeispiel ist eine *infobox* zugeordnet, die eine knappe Definition des jeweiligen Begriffs aus der Perspektive des alltäglichen Gebrauchs liefert. Die Texte sind mehrheitlich den so genannten *serious newspapers* entnommen, während das durchaus typische Beispiel für einen Sensationsbericht *(Mud-Hut-Rat)* aus der *tabloid press* stammt. Besondere Aufmerksamkeit ist bei der Textauswahl auf die hohe Qualität des *comment* und der *column* gelegt worden, weil gerade diese beiden Textsorten zu den hervorstechenden Charakteristika der gehobenen englischen Presselandschaft gehören.

Textsammlungen mit Zeitungsartikeln wird häufig der Vorwurf gemacht, dass ihr thematisches Material schnell veralte und jede inhaltliche Relevanz verliere. Die vorliegende Textsammlung begegnet diesem Vorwurf auf zweierlei Weise: Es sind zum einen Texte zu Ereignissen ausgewählt worden, an die man sich in vielen Jahren erinnern wird und die auch Diskussionsgegenstand bleiben werden (z.B. der Tod von Prinzessin Diana). Zum anderen ist der Versuch unternommen worden Themen auszuwählen, die mehr oder weniger den Charakter des Zeitlosen tragen (z.B. eine *human interest story* wie *Mud-Hut-Rat* oder die Sportreportage *Serene Chang serves the Lord*, die den familiären Hintergrund zweier ganz unterschiedlicher Tennisprofis auf eine Art schildert, die auch dann noch Interesse weckt und Relevanz behält, wenn Michael Chang und David Henman ihre aktive Laufbahn längst beendet haben werden). In wenigen Fällen sind Artikel mit großem Umfang auf ein überschaubares und bearbeitbares Maß gekürzt worden. Ansonsten werden die Texte in ihrer originalen und ursprünglichen Form wiedergegeben.

Die Verfasser vertreten mit Nachdruck die Überzeugung, dass es ein lohnenswertes Ziel für den fortgeschrittenen Lerner im Fach Englisch darstellt, englische Zeitungen nicht nur lesen zu können, sondern die Lektüre auch als eine Form stimulierender gehobener Unterhaltung schätzen zu lernen. Wenn der eine oder andere Schüler nach der Beschäftigung mit diesem Themenheft aus eigener Motivation heraus gelegentlich zu einer englischsprachigen Zeitung greift und diese auch liest, sehen die Verfasser die Ziele dieser Textsammlung als erreicht an.

Das Fernsehen gilt als *das* Medium des späten 20. Jahrhunderts. Fernsehkanäle in englischer Sprache können bereits in vielen deutschen Haushalten empfangen werden. Man darf davon ausgehen, dass in absehbarer Zukunft nahezu jeder einzelne deutsche Bürger Zugang zu solchen Kanälen haben wird. Hier liegt auch der eigentliche Grund dafür, dass bei der Auswahl des Materials kein Versuch unternommen worden ist, Nachrichtensendungen in das zweite Kapitel zu integrieren. Lehrerinnen und Lehrer können problemlos Nachrichtensendungen aufzeichnen und sie unter dem Aspekt der Tagesaktualität im Unterricht besprechen.

Das zweite Kapitel enthält ausschließlich Materialien, die dem britischen Fernsehen entnommen worden sind. Auf den Einbezug medialer Texte aus amerikanischen oder anderen Quellen ist bewusst verzichtet worden. Stattdessen unternimmt die Sammlung den Versuch die besondere Qualität des britischen Fernsehens auf vier unterschiedlichen Gebieten zu dokumentieren: zwei Formen der *situational comedy (sitcom)*, eine Polizeiserie und die Fernsehverfilmung eines literarischen Werkes *(Pride and Prejudice)*.

Alle Beispiele des zweiten Kapitels stießen im Rahmen ihrer Erstaustrahlung auf eine außerordentlich positive Resonanz beim britischen Publikum und haben später auch als Video beachtliche Verkaufserfolge erzielt. Selbst einige Folgen von *The Bill*, der Polizeiserie, sind im Videoformat erhältlich, obwohl die Serie immer noch im Fernsehen läuft.

Transkriptionen von Videomaterial nehmen in der Regel viele Seiten in Anspruch. Es ist daher in dieser Sammlung versucht worden, einen begrenzten, in sich geschlossenen Teilaspekt aus einer Sendung auszuwählen (wie in den Auszügen zu *Fawlty Towers* und *Pride and Prejudice*) oder verschiedene Kurzpassagen durch überbrückende Erläuterungen miteinander zu verbinden, um den Eindruck einer ganzen und inhaltlich geschlossenen Folge zu wecken (wie in den Auszügen zu *The Bill* und *Yes, Prime Minister*).

Schülerinnen und Schüler, die sich mit den Materialien dieser Sammlung gut vertraut gemacht haben, werden feststellen, dass hier eine Grundlage für authentische Kommunikationssituationen mit britischen (aber auch anderen) Muttersprachlern unterschiedlicher Altersgruppen gelegt worden ist. Wohl jeder Großbritannienbesucher macht die Feststellung, dass die Themen und Materialien des zweiten Teils zu integralen Bestandteilen des britischen Alltags geworden sind. Serien wie *Fawlty Towers* oder *Yes, Prime Minister* sind so bekannt, dass man ihnen in ganz unterschiedlichen Bereichen des britischen Lebens begegnen kann, sei es im Rahmen parlamentarischer Debatten, in denen der Name *Sir Humphrey* als Synonym für negative Aspekte des *civil service* ebenso auftaucht wie Zitate wie *Pretentious? Moi?* (see p. 33, l.20) beim Besuch in einem *pub*.

Tabellarische Textübersicht

Text, Autor	Inhaltliche Schwerpunkte	Textsorte	Wortzahl
Chapter 1: English Newspapers			
The facts about ...	Charakteristika der wichtigsten Tages- und Sonntagszeitungen, Unterscheidung zwischen *tabloid-broadsheet/popular-quality newspapers*	Dictionary entry	1190
The Dunblane massacre	Vergleichen und Kontrastieren der Titelseiten einer *tabloid* und drei *broadsheet newspapers* am Tage nach dem Ereignis	Newspaper front page	–
Look back in anger	Den Lesern werden die Ereignisse des 13. März 1966 noch einmal vor Augen geführt. Dabei wird besonders darauf hingewiesen, dass niemand die Absichten Hamiltons vorher wissen konnte. Ebenso wird auf die erfolgreiche Kampagne Handfeuerwaffen zu verbieten verwiesen.	Review article	222
Mud-Hut-Rat; Hilary Douglas	Artikel aus einer *tabloid* um eine englische Hausfrau, die sich während ihres Urlaubs in einen Afrikaner verliebt, Mann und Kinder verlässt und unter primitiven Bedingungen in einem afrikanischen Dorf ein neues Leben beginnen will.	Sensational news story	1092
A princess, a funeral and a nation's sadness	Der Artikel impliziert, dass der Tod von Prinzessin Diana und ihr Begräbnis einfachen Menschen das Gefühl vermittelt habe, ihre Meinungen zählten ebenso wie diejenigen ihrer Herrscher. Die Medien mögen dazu beigetragen haben, den Mythos „der da oben" zerstört zu haben. Langfristig kann diese Überzeugung das Ende der Monarchie bedeuten. Diana selbst wird als 'improbable midwife' einer feministischen Revolution gesehen, die die Briten gelehrt hat ihre Gefühle offen zu zeigen.	Leading article	928

The history of chess ends here, John Lanchester	Kasparovs Niederlage gegen einen Computer bedeutet, dass wir akzeptieren müssen Schach weder als Kunst noch als Sport zu sehen, sondern lediglich als mathematisches Spiel, das Computer besser beherrschen als Menschen.	Comment	613
Manhunt; Andrew Billen	Der Verfasser hatte sein Auto über Nacht auf dem Parkplatz einer Klippe geparkt, während er auf einer mehrtägigen Wanderung unterwegs war. Die Klippe ist auch als Ort für Selbstmorde bekannt. Die anschließende Suche der Polizei stimmt den Verfasser nachdenklich.	Column	537
Giant gates keep sea at bay; Isabel Conway	ein Tatsachenbericht, der mit durchaus dramatischen Akzenten die Vollendung der Sturmbarrieren in den Niederlanden beschreibt.	Factual report	678
Serene Chang serves the Lord; Kevin Mitchell	Der Artikel vergleicht und kontrastiert die völlig unterschiedliche soziale Herkunft und die daraus resultierenden Grundhaltungen der Tennisprofis Michael Chang und Tim Henman.	Sports report	933
Chapter 2: Television			
What's on TV this evening?	Programmübersicht von fünf über Antenne zu empfangende Kanäle	TV programme	1605
Fawlty Towers: The Psychiatrist	Basil Fawlty und seine Frau Sybil führen ein kleines Hotel in Torquay, in dem es recht chaotisch zugeht. Der Auszug unterstreicht Basils snobistische Vorurteile. Seine Haltung gegenüber Mr Johnson (eine Art Playboy, der mit einem Londoner Akzent spricht) ist absolut negativ, während er geradezu unterwürfigen Respekt zwei Doktoren entgegenbringt, die gerade sein Hotel betreten.	Classic TV comedy (sitcom)	774
The Bill	Der Beitrag hat die Rivalität zwischen Detektiven und der uniformierten Polizei an einer Londoner Polizeistation zum Inhalt. Die Rivalität zeigt sich, als sie versuchen einen kleinen Kriminellen, der gerade aus Spanien zurückgekehrt ist, wegen eines Angriffs auf den Liebhaber seiner Frau zu finden und zu verhaften. Der uniformierten Polizei gelingt dies. Gleichzeitig geht ihnen dabei ein gesuchter Drogenhändler ins Netz.	TV police series	2292
Yes, Prime Minister: The Smoke Screen	Dem schwachen Premierminister gelingt einmal ein kleiner Sieg über seinen *Permanent Secretary*, einem einflussreichen, cleveren Beamten. Der Premierminister unterstützt nur scheinbar eine Anti-Raucher-Kampagne seines Gesundheitsministers. Er will eine Steuersenkung durchsetzen um seine Popularität bei den Wählern zu erhöhen. Der Gesundheitsminister kündigt Widerstand an, wird daher ins Finanzministerium versetzt, während der Sportminister, ein Kettenraucher und Lobbyist der Tabakindustrie, Gesundheitsminister wird.	Satirical comedy (sitcom)	2046

Pride and Prejudice	Mr Collins, ein Geistlicher und entfernter Verwandter, besucht die Bennets. Er hat sich entschlossen eine der Töchter zu heiraten. Seine Wahl fällt auf Elizabeth, die ihn nicht ernst nehmen kann, und seinen Antrag ablehnt. Ihre Mutter ist schockiert über ihren Schritt, während ihr Vater sie unterstützt.	TV costume	1979
Postscript: The Media – Watchdog or Rottweiler? Stephen Speight	Informelle Debatte zwischen der Herausgeberin einer *tabloid newspaper*, die ihr Konzept journalistischer Arbeit verteidigt, und einer Gruppe von Schülern, die ihre Berichterstattung wegen ihrer Tendenz zur Sensationslust, der Verletzung der Privatsphäre und fehlender politischer Unabhängigkeit angreift.	Debate	687

Integration des Heftes in größere thematische Zusammenhänge

Die Textauswahl beider Kapitel ist so konzipiert, dass das Heft als Ganzes Gerüst für zwei unterschiedlich ausgerichtete Reihen zum Themenkomplex *Mass Media* Verwendung finden kann. Dabei konzentriert sich eine Reihe auf *English Newspapers*, die andere auf *Television*. Beide Reihen bedürfen indes einer den Interessen und dem Leistungsstand des jeweiligen Kurses angepasste bzw. entsprechende inhaltliche und thematische Ausrichtung in Bezug auf eine exakte Problemformulierung ebenso wie auf eine Bestimmung der methodischen Konzeption im Hinblick auf angestrebte Ziele im Bereich der Arbeits- und Lernorganisation (etwa vor dem Hintergrund der Vertrautheit des Kurses mit Formen der Gruppen- und Partnerarbeit sowie unterschiedlicher Formen der Präsentationstechnik). Diese Schwerpunktsetzungen bestimmen auch den Rahmen für die Auswahl weiterer Unterrichtsmaterialien (Hinweise dazu sind in den Unterrichtsempfehlungen zu finden). Selbstverständlich lässt sich auch aus beiden Kapiteln eine komplexe Reihe zum Themenbereich *Mass Media* gestalten.

Neben diesen offensichtlichen Einsatzmöglichkeiten bietet sich die Sammlung auch für eine weitere Verwendung an. Sie kann über einen längeren Zeitraum als den Unterricht begleitendes Heft im Rahmen inhaltlich und thematisch ganz unterschiedlich orientierter Reihen auszugsweise eingesetzt werden. Dabei sind bsw. folgende thematische Bereiche denkbar:

- Im weiten Themenkomplex *British Politics* sind je nach inhaltlicher Fixierung der Reihe der Artikel zum Tode von Prinzessin Diana (Thema Monarchie) und/oder der Auszug aus *Yes, Prime Minister* gut zu integrieren.
- Eine Reihe zum Problembereich *Human Aggression* kann unter ganz unterschiedlichen Akzenten die Materialien zum *Dunblane massacre* ebenso einsetzen wie den Auszug aus *Fawlty Towers*. Auch *The Bill* lässt sich hier einbringen, wenn die Reihe die Bereiche Kriminalität oder *Law and Order* problematisiert.
- Auch im Rahmen einer Reihe zum weiten Themenkomplex *Aspects of Social Life in GB* kann – wiederum in Abhängigkeit von der für den jeweiligen Kurs fixierten problemorientierten Themenstellung – auf Texte wie *Serene Chang, Mud-Hut-Rat*

ebenso zurückgegriffen werden wie auf *Fawlty Towers* oder – unter Einbezug einer historischen Perspektive – auf den Auszug aus *Pride and Prejudice*.

Aus den vorangegangenen Ausführungen zeichnen sich bereits die thematischen Konturen möglicher Anbindungen des Heftes oder Teile des Heftes an Ganzschriften ab.

Anbindung an Ganzschriften

Vor allem im Bereich der Thematik *British Politics* ergeben sich viele Möglichkeiten der Anbindung. In einigen britischen Romanen der Neunzigerjahre, die z.T. auch in Verfilmung vorliegen, wird das Problem politischer Macht und Moral – auch in Bezug auf die Presse – aus unterschiedlichen Perspektiven thematisiert. Besonders verwiesen sei in diesem Zusammenhang auf die beiden Romane von Michael Dobbs – *The House of Cards* und *To Play the King* (beide bei HarperCollins als Taschenbuch erschienen). Aufstieg und Fall des fiktiven Politikers Francis Urquhart werden eindrucksvoll und spannend dargestellt. Die politische Szene in Westminster wird dabei mit ihren Intrigen und Machtkämpfen, in die auch Pressevertreter involviert sind, realistisch geschildert. Auch Michael Shea durchleuchtet in seinem Roman *Spin Doctor* (erschienen bei HarperCollins) die politische Landschaft im Großbritannien der Jahre nach Thatcher. Am Beispiel der Figur des Dr Mark Ivor, der hinter den Kulissen von Westminster die Strippen britischer Politik zieht, ist neben dem politischen Machtkampf auch die Berichterstattung durch Presse und Fernsehen und deren Manipulation ein Thema. Jonathan Coes im Inhalt komplexe und vielschichtige, im Stil sowohl bittere als auch ironische Auseinandersetzung mit dem Thatcherismus in *What a carve up!* (Penguin, 1995) kann als besonders dankbare Möglichkeit der Anbindung gesehen werden. Coe schildert am Beispiel der fiktiven Familie der Winshaws die unterschiedlichen Karrieren ihrer sechs jüngsten Angehörigen im Großbritannien der Siebziger- bis in die frühen Neunzigerjahre. Trotz des Umfangs kann mit dem Buch deswegen gut gearbeitet werden, weil die einzelnen Handlungsstränge – jeder bezieht sich auf eines der sechs Familienmitglieder – übersichtlich in entsprechend gekennzeichneten Kapiteln verfolgt werden können. Von besonderem Interesse ist dabei die Figur der Hilary, die in Presse und Fernsehen Karriere macht, und an der die Doppelmoral mancher Journalisten eindringlich deutlich wird. Für eine Diskussion des Aspekts der Verantwortung, die Medien in einer demokratischen Gesellschaft zu üben haben, ist dieser Handlungsstrang außerordentlich ergiebig. Auszüge aus dieser aus unterschiedlichen Perspektiven erzählten Geschichte sind für arbeitsteilige Gruppenarbeit mit entsprechenden Präsentationen besonders geeignet.

Hier sei zunächst auf einige (relativ) neue Sachbücher, die wesentliche Informationen zu Presse und Fernsehen in Großbritannien enthalten, verwiesen. Auszüge aus ihnen sind im Übrigen auch als Sachtexte für den Einsatz im Unterricht geeignet.

Weiterführende Literatur

- Curran, James/Seaton, Jean: *Power without Responsibility: The Press and Broadcasting in Britain*; London: Routledge, 1991, pp. 429

- Masterman, Len: *Teaching about Television*; Basingstoke: Macmillan 1980; repr. 1993, pp. 222
- McQueen, David: *Television – A Media Student's Guide*; London: Hodder Headline 1998, pp. 274

Hinweise zur methodischen Gestaltung des Unterrichts finden sich in:
- Bach, G./J.-P. Timm (Hrsg.): *Englischunterricht*; Tübingen: A. Francke Verlag 1996, 2. Aufl., pp. 334
- Timm, Johannes-P.: *Englisch lernen und lehren. Didaktik des Englischunterrichts*; Berlin: Cornelsen 1998, pp. 432

Teil II

Discover ... English Newspapers and Television: Das Schülerbuch im Unterricht

Chapter 1: **Newspapers**

Vorbemerkungen zum Kapitel

Für die Arbeit im Kursverband hängt die Reihenfolge, in der die Texte gelesen und bearbeitet werden, von der jeweiligen inhaltlichen und thematischen Schwerpunktsetzung, wie sie von Fachlehrer und -lehrerin mit dem Kurs vereinbart worden sind, ab. Sollte das Kapitel als Ganzes bearbeitet werden, empfiehlt sich die Reihenfolge des Schülerbandes.

Start here

About the photographs

The photographs show two ways in which newspapers are sold, give some idea of the huge diversity of newspaper and magazine production, and show something of the drama of the newspaper business.

Unterrichtsempfehlungen

Die Bilder gehen vom Endprodukt, dem individuellen Zeitungsexemplar, aus. In Deutschland erhalten die meisten Haushalte die regionale Tageszeitung ins Haus geliefert, während ein Teil der Leser eine Zeitung am Kiosk ersteht. Es erscheint ergiebig, mit einem Kurs den gemeinsamen Versuch zu unternehmen den komplexen Produktionsprozess einer Tageszeitung zu rekonstruieren. Dies lässt sich durchaus im rückwärtigen Verfahren vornehmen; d.h. man unternimmt den Prozess beginnend mit dem Endabnehmer, der Verteilerkette, dem Versand von der Druckerei, dem Druckprozess etc. Ziel dieser Besprechung ist es, die diffzile logistische Operation zu verdeutlichen, die jeden Abend und jede Nacht bei einer Zeitung reibungslos ablaufen muss, damit die Exemplare rechtzeitig ihre Abnehmer erreichen. Bei rechtzeitiger Planung der Reihe kann überlegt werden, ob (u.U. gemeinsam mit einem Deutschkurs) ein Besuch bei einer Zeitung möglich ist, um sich diesen Prozess näher erläutern zu lassen. Im Englischkurs kann anschließend das Ergebnis in unterschiedlicher Form (im Kursverband, in Gruppenarbeit zu Hause) in der Zielsprache ausgewertet werden. Hier bietet sich auch die Möglichkeit einer sinnvollen Wortschatzarbeit in Bezug auf fachsprachliche Aspekte der Zeitungsproduktion.

It's all in the newspapers p. 5

Try to decide where each of these pictures was taken. Why do you think there is still so much interest in newspapers and magazines in the electronic age? Most people would find the picture of the newspaper presses in action quite dramatic. Why might this be?

First picture – a newsstand, possibly in an international setting such as an airport
Second picture – presses rolling, inside the printing works of a newspaper

Third picture – a street newspaper vendor outside a public building (possibly a bank) which is not open on Sunday (he is selling Sunday newspapers)

There is still a great deal of interest in printed newspapers and magazines because displaying and reading such publications on a computer screen is not something the majority of people want to do or are capable of doing (yet). It is not as easy (yet) to read (and/or print) text from a computer as it is from a printed page/newspaper/magazine.

The layout of "real" magazines and newspapers is still more sophisticated than screen layouts. Complicated electronic layouts usually take a long time to build up on the screen.

The picture of the presses in action is dramatic because we can imagine thousands, even millions of copies being run off in the course of a few hours, and transported to every corner of the country by breakfast time (one of the great steps forward in the distribution of information which arrived with the railways).

The facts about ...

About the text

There has been no attempt to include all the daily and Sunday newspapers, but typical features of all the main publications are at least mentioned. Pupils should choose three or four representative newspapers for their charts rather than trying to cover them all.

Synopsis of the text

The material covers the entire press landscape in England in compact form. It mentions the popularity of both daily and Sunday newspapers, and makes the important distinction between quality and popular newspapers. Characteristics of some of the most important newspapers such as The Times are given individually, while other newspapers, particularly the popular or tabloid newspapers, are dealt with on a group basis apart from the two most important tabloids, The Sun and the Daily Mirror. Middle market newspapers and regional or local newspapers are also covered. There is a brief account of the role played by proprietors.

Unterrichtsempfehlungen

Zur sprachlichen wie inhaltlichen Erarbeitung der *facts about ...* empfiehlt es sich, als einleitenden Schritt im Sinne einer Hinführung zum Thema eine kurze Skizzierung der deutschen Presselandschaft mit den ihr eigenen Charakteristika vorauszuschicken (z.B. überregionale Zeitungen, regionale Zeitungen mit Lokalteil, die Rolle der *Bildzeitung*, Sonntagszeitungen, das Problem der politischen Einflussnahme durch die Eigentümer), die dann im weiteren Verlauf der unterrichtlichen Erarbeitung als Folie für eine kontrastive Betrachtung der britischen Presse dienen können. Hier wird inhaltlich auf entsprechendes Vorwissen der Schüler und Schülerinnen zurückgegriffen. Diese Phase lässt sich unterschiedlich gestalten. Kenntnisse können durch Sammeln in Form eines *brainstorming* an der Tafel oder auf dem OHP festgehalten werden. Alternativ geben Partner- bzw. Gruppenarbeitsformen einen Rahmen für ein sinnvolles Zusammentragen von Vorwissen. Im Sinne der Zeitökonomie erscheint eine die Arbeit der einzelnen Gruppen steuernde Aufgabenstellung sinnvoll, die damit auch die anschließende Auswertungsphase strukturiert. Auf der Ebene der Lexik ermöglicht eine solche Phase dem Fachlehrer/der Fachlehrerin eine präzisere Bestimmung des Kenntnisstandes in Bezug auf den Grad der Beherrschung bereits vorauszusetzender Teile des Fachvokabulars. Somit lassen sich im Zusammenhang der Skizzierung der deutschen Presse eventuelle Desiderate im Bereich der Lexik aufarbeiten.

In einem zweiten Schritt werden bereits vorhandene Kenntnisse über die britische Presse gesammelt. Dabei dürften in den Kursgruppen zumindest eine Reihe isolierter Einzelaspekte vorgetragen werden, die im Rahmen des Unterrichts in der Sek. I, aus der tagespolitischen Beobachtung (etwa in der Auseinandersetzung um das britische Königshaus und den Tod von Prinzessin Diana) sowie u.U. aus erster unmittelbarer Leseerfahrung im Zusammenhang eines Aufenthaltes im Land der Zielsprache gewonnen wurden und reaktivierbar sind. Während der erste Schritt versucht zu einer zumindest in groben Zügen systematisierten Darstellung der deutschen Tages- und Wochenpresse zu gelangen, geht es in diesem zweiten Schritt lediglich um ein spontanes Anführen von Kenntnissen und Erfahrungen, ohne dass eine weitere Systematisierung erforderlich scheint. Dies wird auch im unterschiedlich abzusteckenden zeitlichen Rahmen für die beiden Vorhaben deutlich. Dabei kann der erste durchaus eine ganze Unterrichtsstunde in Anspruch nehmen, der zweite jedoch nur zwischen fünf bis zehn Minuten.

Die Arbeit mit den einzelnen Texten zu *The facts about ...* eignet sich besonders für die Schulung des intensiven Lesens und des gezielten Extrapolierens bestimmter inhaltlicher Aspekte, wie sie die tabellarische Übersicht auf Seite 7 vorgibt. Der dort vorgegebene Kriterienkatalog lässt sich gemeinsam mit dem Kurs erweitern (z.B.: *political views/tendencies; character of the paper: national, regional*). Die Erarbeitung der Texte kann auf zwei unterschiedlichen Wegen erfolgen: Die Texte werden von allen Kursteilnehmern gelesen und die Ergebnisse im Anschluss gemeinsam ausgewertet und an der Tafel oder auf Folie fixiert. Abwechslungsreicher, die Schüler und Schülerinnen stärker fordernder und u.U. auch zeitökonomischer mag der zweite Weg sein: In Partnerarbeit setzen sich je zwei Schüler und Schülerinnen mit jeweils drei Texten auseinander. Sie sind verpflichtet ihren Teil des Textkorpus für den gesamten Kurs sorgfältig zu untersuchen und vorzustellen. So kann im Rahmen der anschließenden Auswertung eines jeden Textes auf die Arbeitsergebnisse mehrerer Gruppen zurückgegriffen werden. Diese Phase dürfte damit vom Zeitablauf her zügig und vom Inhalt her durch die Möglichkeit, bei eventuell erforderlichen Korrekturen und Ergänzungen auf die anderen Gruppen zurückgreifen zu können, auch abgesicherter verlaufen.

Assignments

What are the main characteristics of these newspapers? Put your findings in a chart like this.

◀ p. 7

	The Times	Daily Telegraph	The Sun
Tabloid or Broadsheet?	Broadsheet	Broadsheet	Broadsheet
Founded?	1785	1855	1964
Contents?	extensive news coverage, letters, financial and sports news, crossword	detailed reporting, international news sports	personal aspects of news, scandals, sensations etc., Royal family
Use of photos?	usually sparing, not very large	as for Times	a lot of large, dramatic photos
Type of reader?	well-educated, prosperous, right of centre	similar to Times but older readers on the whole	less demanding, less well-educated readers, not very interested in politics
Circulation?	c. 500,000	c. 1,000,000	c. 4,000,000

(Information on other newspapers also available in the text)

The Dunblane massacre

Pupils should only compare titles, headlines and photographs here. It is not intended that they should try to read the small print.

Die Beschäftigung mit dem *Dunblane Massacre* ist im weiteren Kontext des Themenkomplexes *Aggression* zu sehen und kann daher auch isoliert in eine Unterrichtssequenz integriert werden, die anhand von Texten unterschiedlichen Formats das Gewaltphänomen in unserer Gegenwart thematisiert. Im Einzelnen schult die Aufgabe insbesondere den kritischen Umgang mit Bildmaterial in Verbindung mit Text. Sie erlaubt ebenfalls den ersten Transfer inhaltlicher Kenntnisse aus den *facts about* (S. 6f.) auf die Erschießung des Bild- und Textmaterials, insbesondere auf bestimmte Merkmale der Schlagzeilengestaltung, wie sie für einzelne Zeitungen typisch erscheinen. Insgesamt stellt die Auseinandersetzung mit diesen Seiten hohe Anforderungen an die Schüler und Schülerinnen, weil sie die Schulung des kritischen Umgangs mit der Presse und den je nach Charakter der Zeitung unterschiedlichen Konventionen ihrer Berichterstattung an einen emotional außerordentlich befrachteten Kontext bindet. Vor der inhaltlichen Auseinandersetzung mit den Fotos und der Diskussion des Arbeitsauftrages auf Seite 10 oben kann über die Problematik des Waffenbesitzes auf die Thematik hingearbeitet werden (z.B. *Is the ownership of a gun already an invitation to a criminal act?*). Mithilfe einer solchen Hinführung wird ein Mei-

About the title pages

Unterrichts-empfehlungen

nungsbild erstellt, auf das u.U. im Anschluss an die Erschließungsarbeit der Fotos wie des Zeitungsartikels zurückgegriffen werden kann, um es vor dem Hintergrund neu erworbener Kenntnisse über das Massaker zu überdenken und ggf. zu revidieren.

Die Darstellung des tragischen Ereignisses von Dunblane in der britischen Presse zeigt markante Unterschiede in der Berichterstattung zwischen *tabloid* und *serious newspapers* auf. Alle vier Zeitungen drucken dasselbe Klassenphoto und eine Abbildung des Täters. Die *serious papers* konzentrieren sich daneben auf eine textliche Darstellung des Ereignisses, während demgegenüber die *Sun* schon in der Schlagzeile emotional reagiert. Auffällig ist auch der reißerische Hinweis unten auf der Seite, dass auf weiteren 18 Seiten das tragische Ereignis dargestellt wird. Dieser Hinweis ist wohl von Verkaufsabsichten geprägt und schlachtet das verbreitete Interesse an Sensationsnachrichten kommerziell aus.

Im Anschluss an diese Besprechung im Kursverband sollte unmittelbar auf den *review article* zu diesem Thema übergeleitet werden. Verbinden lässt sich dies mit der spekulativen Frage, wie ein Journalist angesichts eines solchen Ereignisses seinen Artikel gestalten könnte.

Assignments

Pre-reading task

Comparing headlines p. 8

Which of the newspapers in the montage do you think are "popular", and which are "serious"? Give reasons for your answers. The fact box will help you.

> *The Sun* is clearly popular:
> - tabloid format
> - large headline
> - very large photograph
> - brief text
> - emotive language
>
> *The Telegraph*, *Times* and *Independent* are all serious:
> - broadsheet format
> - The *Telegraph* has a restrained headline, but the other two papers have gone for emotive and dramatic headlines on this occasion.
> - smaller photographs
> - longer texts in smaller type

Additional Assignment

Students could be asked to buy several different German (and if possible British) daily newspapers on a day when a major news story dominates the headlines, and compare English and German approaches to the news.

A review article:
Look back in anger

About the text

It is worth emphasising that this article appeared as part of a survey of the year's events in December 1966, nine months after the massacre itself and the publication of the newspapers which appear on the previous pages. In the meantime the shock will have worn off, at least for those not directly involved, but the massacre will inevitably have stayed in people's minds as one of the most striking events of the year. The parents launched a very effective campaign to have handguns banned, and because there was almost 100% support for a ban, draconian laws were passed remarkably quickly. Although the writer says "we will never know why he did it", it became clear after the event that Hamilton was a social outcast and gun freak, who possessed an arsenal of legally registered firearms. He was suspected of pedophile tendencies and had recently been banned from voluntary work with teenage boys.

Synopsis of the text

People in Britain remember where they were when they heard the first news of the tragedy, and later the full horror of the news that sixteen small children and their teacher had been killed by a deranged local man in Dunblane, Scotland. However, the murderer, Thomas Hamilton, did not appear to be mad in photographs. He did not behave in an unusual way even on the morning of the killings. As he committed suicide after the shootings, we will never know his true motives. Although local people thought he was odd, nobody could have guessed that he was capable of such a terrible act. It was right of the Dunblane parents to press for a ban on handguns. The new laws will make another Dunblane a lot less likely.

Unterrichts-empfehlungen

Den o.a. Anmerkungen zu den Abbildungen der unterschiedlichen Titelseiten ist der Hinweis zu entnehmen Bildmaterial und Text im Rahmen **einer** Unterrichtseinheit zu behandeln. Die Beschäftigung mit dem *review article* knüpft damit an die beschreibende Auseinandersetzung mit den Titelseiten der vier Zeitungen an (s.o.). Der Text kann in Stillarbeit gelesen werden, wobei die Schülerinnen und Schüler bei der Lektüre bereits den ersten der beiden Arbeitsaufträge vorbereiten. U.U. kann anschließend vor der zweiten Aufgabe die Frage besprochen werden, ob die Form der Darstellung der Tragik des Ereignisses gerecht wird. Die abschließende Aufgabenstellung schließt das Thema *Dunblane massacre* ab. Die Diskussion kann von Lehrerseite eingeleitet werden mit dem Hinweis auf die vom britischen Parlament als Folge dieses Ereignisses vollzogenen gesetzgeberischen Maßnahmen (Einziehung von Handfeuerwaffen; allgemeines Verbot des Waffenbesitzes bei nur wenigen Ausnahmen unter strengen Sicherheitsauflagen). Die Schülerinnen und Schüler können auf die Situation in Deutschland verweisen. Auch Hinweise auf den gegenwärtigen Diskussionsstand zum Thema Waffenbesitz in den U.S.A., wo extreme Gegensätze aufeinander prallen und Waffenbesitz von einigen Verfechtern als Ausdruck eines fundamentalen Menschenrechts gesehen wird, kann zusätzliche Impulse in diese Diskussion geben.

Assignments

Pre-reading task

p. 10 All the newspaper headlines on the previous two pages appeared on March 14 1996, the day after the Dunblane Massacre. Try to find similarities and differences between the various headlines. What is your first reaction to the events described?

Similarities and differences:
The *Independent* and *The Times* have chosen very similar headlines, of a type which would normally be more typical for a tabloid newspaper. *The Telegraph* is more restrained.
The *Sun* has chosen a pseudo-religious headline for maximum emotional impact, but cannot resist using the word *massacre* in a smaller headline.
First reactions are likely to be shock, outrage, and, inevitably, curiosity – the wish to find out more.
Normally there would be a wish for justice, even revenge, as far as the killer is concerned, but this will turn out to be inappropriate here because the murderer committed suicide at the scene of the crime.

Activities

The Dunblane massacre p. 10

1. Using the information in the text and the headlines, try to piece together what happened on that day, and write a brief, factual report.

The day started normally for Thomas Hamilton. He said hello to neighbours as he scraped the ice off his windscreen. They did not know that he had guns in his car, and was about to go to the local school with the intention of shooting as many children as possible. He drove to the school and started shooting in Class P1. The teacher tried to protect the children, and was killed herself. By the time the police and ambulances had arrived, sixteen children and their teacher were dead or dying. The murderer had committed suicide by shooting himself.

2. Why do you think people occasionally go berserk, as Hamilton did? What kind of person could he have been, and how might the community have treated him?

See the information at the end of *About the text*.

Additional Assignment

It would be interesting do do some brainstorming here. Ask the class what national or international events have made an exceptional impact on people in Germany in recent years. What factors make an event particularly memorable (distance from home – the nearer the more memorable, numbers of people involved – particularly horrible crime/tragedy – event of historic significance such as reunification.) As a starter the class could discuss the joke headline: SMALL EARTHQUAKE IN MONGOLIA. FEW INJURED.

A sensational news story:
Mud-Hut-Rat Hilary Douglas

About the text

The contrast between 'primitive' life in Africa and 'civilised' life in Britain is almost too good to be true and definitely racist. On the other hand, these elements, plus the contrast between the erotic African lover and the English husband who took his wife for granted make the story interesting to read, and very likely to appeal to a typical tabloid reader, perhaps to most people, although readers used to broadsheet newspapers would object to the style and probably feel sceptical about some parts of the story.

The pre-reading activity will help students to see this story as a typical, even "classic" tabloid story. Features which should emerge during the discussion:

'good story':
human interest, sex and other 'juicy' details, clear story line, plenty of quotations, an element of expectation – in this case the 'eternal triangle' element with two contrasting lovers and life-styles

packaging:
large headlines, large and/or heavy type near the beginning, photographs, sub-headings, use of emotive, in this case even racist language. Pandering to the assumed tastes and prejudices of the reader.

Synopsis of the text

The article from *The Sun* is written in standard tabloid style by a competent journalist, Hilary Douglas. The article describes how the wife of a businessman fell in love with an African while she was on holiday in Gambia.

She returned home with her husband, confessed that she had made love to the African, then returned to live with him on a permanent basis, leaving the husband "heartbroken".

The husband felt that his wife had lost all sense of reality because of the flattery she received from her African lover, and found it hard to believe that she had chosen to live in squalor. He had no intention of taking her back and was trying to bury himself in his business.

The wife saw her situation as very romantic and felt that she was living in a paradise on earth. Sunshine and sex more than compensated for the lack of running water and a cesspit as a toilet.

It was love at first sight, when the wife saw the African riding towards her along the beach. The couple have opened a riding school together. The wife's only regret was that she was separated from her children. She felt that she had to take her chance of real happiness.

Unterrichts-empfehlungen

Die Attraktion von Sensationsberichten in der Presse wie im Fernsehen ist ungebrochen. Es ist daher sinnvoll, im Rahmen von Unterrichtssequenzen zur Presse wie zur kritischen Medienerziehung auf diese Thematik näher einzugehen. Hier lässt sich eine Analyse des spezifischen Textformats solcher Berichte gezielt verorten und in Bezug auf thematische Horizonte, Darstellungsformen und Sprache bestimmen.

Dieser für das typische *tabloid*-Format schon umfangreiche Bericht eignet sich für diese Aufgaben, weil sich an ihm wesentliche Aspekte des Sensationsberichts exemplifizieren lassen, auf die der Aufgabenapparat auf der Seite 13 zugeschnitten ist.

Im Anschluss an die *pre-reading task* wird der Text in Kleingruppen anhand der 3 Arbeitsaufträge erschlossen. Damit gibt es neben der inhaltlichen auch eine methodische Akzentsetzung insofern, als dass AG ihre Ergebnisse ganz oder teilweise dem Plenum präsentieren. Wichtig ist in diesem Zusammenhang die Festlegung der Kriterien für die Ergebnispräsentation: lediglich ein Festhalten von Stichworten auf Folie um freies Sprechen zu üben und den Blickkontakt zur Gruppe zu halten; die strukturierte Anlage – mit Einleitung, Anführen der erarbeiteten Aspekte und einem abrundenden Schlussgedanken. Es sollte ausreichend Zeit für diese Phase zur Verfügung gestellt werden um mehrere Gruppen zu Wort kommen zu lassen und deren Ergebnisse abschließend zu diskutieren. Je nach Erfahrung der Gruppe mit der Präsentation solcher Ergebnisse ist auch eine Auswertung dieser Phase unter methodischem Aspekt sinnvoll.

Assignments

Pre-reading task

Before you read ▶
p. 11

Do a bit of brain-storming based on the title. What kind of story do you expect? How about the "plot"? What kind of style will the journalist probably employ? What sort of details do you expect?

Students could be expected to refer to a mud-hut as the home of a "native" in Africa (prejudiced view, cliché). They should guess that the plot will be based on the so-called eternal triangle – in this case one woman and two men. They will need words such as sexy, sensational, juicy, emotive language, racist overtones to describe the style. The details are likely to be intimate, personal, referring to sex, contrasting life in Africa with life in Britain.

Activities

The popular press ▶
p. 13

1. What features of this article are typical for an article in a popular newspaper? Cover the story itself, the headlines, the layout and the choice of vocabulary.

Students should mention large headlines, large and/or heavy type near the beginning, photographs, sub-headings, use of emotive, in this case even racist language, pandering to the assumed tastes and prejudices of the reader.

2. Some of the vocabulary used could be described as racist and/or prejudiced. Pick out some words and expressions of

this kind and look them up in a good dictionary. Comment on the use of this kind of vocabulary in a large-circulation newspaper.

e.g. mud-hut, rat, primitive (hut), squalor, terrified of AIDS, out for what he can get. Learners should comment that it is irresponsible for a newspaper to use this kind of vocabulary because it may encourage readers to feel that it is acceptable for them to speak in this way too, and even lead to an increase in racist views and behaviour.

3. Most people would find the article interesting, even if they disapproved of it. How do journalists try to keep the reader's interest?

See notes on the pre-reading task. Students should be reminded that they should give examples when answering a question of this kind. Examples for arousing and keeping interest:
- first two sentences – emotive language, e.g. heartbroken, dumped, mud-hut, native, black hunk, romantic ... trip.
- Some key facts given at the beginning, reader's appetite is whetted – wants to know more.
- Use of italics for dramatic parts of the story.
- Switch of viewpoint to the runaway wife in Africa.
- Local colour, e.g. Stirring a pot on an open fire outside the shack she now calls home.

Write a short summary of the article, just giving the main facts. Compare your summary with the original. What is missing? Which is more objective? Which is more fun to read? Give reasons for your answers.

◀ **Summarising the article** p. 13

See the synopsis. Missing elements are likely to be the juicy details, most of the direct speech, elements of repetition. No doubt the original will be more fun to read.

Can you write a newspaper article ...

◀ **Writing a newspaper article** p. 13

Students who follow the guidelines will produce credible newspaper stories, and at the same time discover how this kind of text is constructed – learning by doing.

A few years ago *The Guardian* decided to print a popular newspaper which did not rely on Sport, Sex and Sensations (the 3 S's) to win readers ...

◀ **Something to think about** p. 13

Some students might like to try writing an exciting news story from British or German newspapers in 3 different ways:
- tabloid sensational – see Activities 1
- tabloid respectable – similar, but with racism and sensationalism less blatant – see the note in the pupil's book.
- broadsheet – smaller headlines, factual report without emotive language, emphasis on consequences for the children, questions asked about whether the wife will tire of her new life sooner or later.

The results could be compared. Particularly suitable for computer enthusiasts who will be able to produce very realistic layouts.

A leading article: *A princess, a funeral and a nation's sadness*

Author

There is no author's name attached to the article, as is usual with a leading article. We can assume that it was written by senior editorial staff.

About the text

The appearance of this text in a normally level-headed newspaper is surprising. It is clear that whoever wrote it was overwhelmed by the national sense of mouring which swept the country after Princess Diana's death. It bears witness to the strength of this feeling, but a few months or years later things have inevitably quietened down.

However, the feeling that things are changing in Britain persists. A Labour government is in power with a huge majority, and likely to remain there for a long time unless it makes disastrous mistakes. The royal family is seen as having lost the jewel in its crown, although in a sense Princess Diana was no longer fully part of it after her divorce.

As Britain moved into 1998 it became clear that changes would not be as radical as had been expected. For example, reform of the House of Lords and the abolition of fox-hunting were put on the back burner. Major efforts were made to improve the National Health Service and the quality of state education, but there was no sign of any attempt to reform or abolish the blatantly élitist public (ie. private, fee-paying) schools. Benefits to single mothers were actually cut – a surprising tactical blunder by Labour politicians, whose party is traditionally seen as the champion of the disadvantaged. The Royal Family kept a low profile and began to enjoy rather more respect and sympathy than it had received immediately after Diana's fatal accident.

Synopsis of the text

The article begins by pointing out that the week after the death of Princess Diana in a car accident must have been very difficult for her two sons, and even more difficult for Prince Charles. The huge outpouring of public emotion at the funeral is described as "a uniquely democratic event" which paradoxically threatened the monarchy. The palace seriously misjudged the public mood at first, and was forced to share in the collective mourning in a more obvious way.

Ordinary people now know more than ever before about the lives of the famous. The other side of the coin is a new confidence among ordinary people that their opinions are worth as much as anybody else's. The traditional deference of people in Britain towards those who used to be called their "betters" has completely disappeared.

Reasons for this change are that the media have destroyed the mystique of those in high places, comprehensive education has produced people with egalitarian values, and women are playing a much more important role in society. People, even members of the élite, are generally unsure of their values nowadays.

Mr Blair's victory in May 1997 can be seen as part of a trend towards a more egalitarian society which became obvious to everyone after Diana's death. The future role of the monarchy in such a society is uncertain. The way that the British legal system operates to the advantage of the powerful and limits freedom of information is now out of date.

Diana's beauty and grace complemented her other, essentially feminine emotional abilities She can be seen as the improbable midwife to the feminist revolution which has now come of age.

Unterrichts-empfehlungen

Abgesehen vom funktionalen Aspekt der Textsorte lässt sich die unterrichtliche Beschäftigung mit diesem Text vor dem Hintergrund der Rekonstruktion des eigenen Erlebens von Dianas Todesfall situieren. So kann die emotional aufgeladene Atmosphäre jener Tage als Hintergrund dienen, vor dem aus der Text mit dem Fragenapparat bearbeitet werden kann.

Darüber hinaus wird der Text zur Folie, vor der inzwischen erfolgte Entwicklungen in diesem Themenkomplex, die hier nicht vorweggenommen werden können, angesprochen werden. Damit rücken Fragestellungen in den Vordergrund wie z.B.: hat die zeitliche Distanz die Reaktion auf Dianas Tod entemotionalisiert, sind im Text angesprochene mögliche Entwicklungen eingetreten und dort angekündigte Konsequenzen für die Stellung und das Ansehen der Monarchie als Tendenzen erkennbar? Die Diskussion im Plenum kann dabei auch Aspekte wie die Entwicklung der Persönlichkeit von Prinz Charles und der beiden Söhne, das Verhalten der Presse gegenüber Persönlichkeiten des öffentlichen Lebens einbeziehen wie auch mögliche Veränderungen gegenüber der Person von Prinzessin Diana. Damit wird deutlich, dass dieser Text auch jenseits eines primär funktionalen Kontextes unter der Fragestellung *What is a leading article?* unter unterschiedlichen thematischen Schwerpunktsetzungen (Entwicklung der Monarchie; Rolle der Presse; Idealisierung einzelner Menschen durch die breite Öffentlichkeit) herangezogen werden kann. Dieser Einbezug des unmittelbaren Entwicklungsstandes zum Zeitpunkt der jeweiligen Lektüre bietet unterrichtsmethodisch Möglichkeiten Kursmitglieder bei der Vorbereitung und Gestaltung der Stunden zu dieser Thematik einzubinden. Sie können im Rahmen von Referaten Informationen zu diesen Themenbereichen aus unterschiedlichen Medien für eine Präsentation vorbereiten. Auf diese Weise kann der Kurs im Plenum diese Informationen gemeinsam auswerten und – je nach der inhaltlichen Schwerpunktsetzung der Unterrichtsreihe – den jeweiligen Entwicklungsstand skizzieren und vor dem Hintergrund des Textes interpretieren. So werden die Konsequenzen von Dianas Unfalltod, seien sie politischer oder anderer Art, zeitkritisch betrachtet.

Assignments

Pre-reading task

How do people react to the death of a really famous and much-loved person? Is there a danger of over-reaction? Does it make

◀ Before you read p. 14

sense that millions of people still mourn for Elvis Presley, for example? Should we feel sorry for them? What is your spontaneous reaction to the photographs printed above?

Sense of outrage, unwillingness to believe that the person is really dead, conspiracy theories, public mourning on a very wide scale, souvenir-collecting, start of an "industry" based on the dead person, either commercially motivated or, as in Diana's case, with charitable intentions.
Spontaneous reactions to the photographs could be:
contrast between the living princess and her mourning relatives, the shock effect of the wrecked car and the knowledge that people died inside it, huge scale of the floral tributes, speculation about Prince Charles's thoughts in view of the fact that his married life with Princess Diana had in fact ended some time before.

While-reading tasks

▶ p. 15 Why exactly was taking part in Diana's funeral procession so difficult for Prince Charles?

Because he was expected to be the leading mourner although Diana was no longer his wife, and he may no longer have felt any love for her.

▶ p. 15 When you have read to the end of the article, try to explain the paradox referred to here.

The paradox lies in the fact that the death of a princess, someone at the very top of the social scale, seems to have been most powerfully felt by ordinary people, who brought pressure on the queen to share in the national mourning in a more obvious way.

▶ p. 15 What is the difference between a *citizen* and a *subject*?

A citizen has more rights than a subject, who is definitely seen as subordinate to e.g. a king or queen.
First meanings in the Collins English Dictionary (Glasgow: HarperCollins, 1991³):
Citizen: a ... member of a state, nation, or other political community.
Subject: a person who lives under the rule of a monarch, government etc.
Note that there is no mention of subordination in the case of *citizen*. The queen is a citizen, too!

▶ p. 16 Why is Diana referred to as an *improbable midwife* for the feminist revolution?

Points that could be made:
- believed in feminine charm, dressing smartly etc.
- seemed on the whole to accept the role of wife and mother
- ability to empathise, feel etc. usually seen as feminine rather than feminist attributes
- (not in article but relevant) worked in a kindergarten before her marriage – hardly a serious career.

Activities

1. "The crown must follow where the people lead." What evidence for this statement does the writer find in the events surrounding Princess Diana's funeral?

◀ **Interpreting the text p. 17**

The funeral itself had popular elements, such as the song sung by Elton John.
The public insisted on the right to participate in the mourning.
The Palace wanted to stay aloof from the nationwide mourning, but public pressure forced them to share in it.

2. Princess Diana is referred to as prime *exponent ... prisoner ...* and *victim* of a culture where people think they have "the right to know intimate personal details of those in public life." Discuss the implications of each of the three terms.

prime exponent:
seen as someone who played up to the media, made sure she photographed well, and enjoyed basking in the spotlight of publicity most of the time. She was prepared to share intimate thoughts about her failed marriage etc. with the public in a television interview.
prisoner:
unable to live a normal life because of press harassment of an extreme kind (even photographed while doing fitness training in a private gymnasium).
victim:
actually died while trying to escape from a group of motorised journalists and paparazzi. More general point that she encouraged media attention, but then found that she could not "turn it on and off" when she wanted to.

3. The writer mentions three factors leading to a loss of "deference to those higher in the social scale" and the disappearance of "stoical acceptance of the status quo" among ordinary British people. Outline each of the three factors briefly in your own words.

- Media attention and intrusion into their private lives has more or less destroyed the mystique of the royals and other famous people.
- comprehensive education has produced a generation of people who believe in equality (a fact which the privately-educated élite has not yet grasped)
- women are playing a much more important part in British life and culture.

4. How exactly may the life and untimely death of Princess Diana threaten the Royal family?

This question requires the student to think in general terms about the article. The following points could be made:
- Diana by far the most popular member of the royal family.
- Prince Charles not very popular – some people think Prince William should become king when he is old enough. No precedent for this – could threaten the monarchy.

- People turning against a hereditary monarchy as part of a general trend towards more equality, accelerated by reactions to Diana's death
- Ordinary people have discovered that they have more power than they might once have thought.

Views of the monarchy p. 17

The writer clearly feels that the British monarchy may be coming to an end. Argue the case for and against a monarchy, making your own views clear.

Standard debating points on both sides:

for	against
hereditary principle clearly understood	reinforces class distinction
usually have star quality/glamour	supports an anachronistic peerage/ House of Lords
well-known in other countries	Monarch not necessarily good at the job, hardworking or attractive to his/her subjects
many ordinary people like to look up to them – proud of having a royal family – follow their lives in newspapers and magazines, feel real loyalty towards them, particularly in times of national crisis (both world wars).	disgraceful behaviour by some members of the royal family
	danger of arrogance, royal family legitimises private education, hunting, all kinds of exclusiveness (e.g. royal enclosures at racecourses, royal garden parties etc.)
Presidents often dull	
Hard to find a generally acceptable choice.	

Overreaction? p. 17

The following text is an extract from an article by Richard Ingrams, published in the same edition of *The Observer* as the leading article above. When you have read it, try to decide where your own sympathies lie. Prepare a short personal statement and read it out to the class. Talk about the different viewpoints which emerge.

Points which could be made:

Overreaction – yes
Most mourners did not know the princess personally.
She was involved in an affair with an "unsuitable" playboy
She herself did not deserve such tremendous popularity before and after her death – in many ways quite an ordinary person
Brought most of her problems on herself
Reactions a kind of mass hysteria
Ambivalent attitude to the media – she courted journalists and paparazzi – and tried to get away from them.

Overreaction – no
She was the only really popular member of the royal family
Truly glamorous, real star quality. She really seemed to care about ordinary people, victims of landmines etc.
Death particularly tragic – still young and beautiful, princes have lost their mother.
Feelings of ordinary people were genuine – why not show them.
Mourners set an example to the royal family.
People wanted to show the other royals how much they loved Diana

A comment: *The history of chess ends here* John Lanchester

About the text

This text was selected because it brings home to readers the fact that machines in general and computers in particular are gradually taking over more and more activities which were seen in the past as the exclusive province of human beings.
The dramatic defeat of Kasparov in 1997 can be seen as a turning point. We have been forced to admit that the game of chess is entirely mathematical, and that computers are better at this kind of mathematics than the world's best chess player. Not everyone will share the author's view that we need not fear computer encroachment into the realms of consciousness and true creative activity.

Synopsis of the text

Chess has in the past usually been seen as an art or a sport, even a violent sport. The game is beautiful in the way that mathematics is beautiful, but also ugly, because players make mistakes and miss chances. Great games can be replayed and appreciated in the same way that art can be appreciated.
However, Kasparov's defeat by a computer called Deep Blue seems to suggest that chess is just a game after all, and a game that can be won by "raw computational power". It would be nice if we could still believe that human intuition counts for something, but unfortunately this is not the case.
The writer feels that the history of chess has to some extent come to an end, now that we know computers can play the game better than we can. This is sad, but it does not mean that computers will now start to do other things better than humans. They do not possess general intelligence, have not developed consciousness, and they cannot create true art.
The defeat of the world's best chess player by a machine is nevertheless bad news for the human race.

Unterrichts- empfehlungen

Ein möglicher inhaltlicher Ansatz für die Auseinandersetzung mit diesem Text ist dessen Einbettung in die Diskussion über die Rolle der Technologie im Spannungsfeld zwischen den Polen der Verherrlichung einerseits und Verteufelung andererseits. Der Text lässt sich über die Bearbeitung der beiden Aufgaben des Apparates inhaltlich erschließen, wobei die zweite Aufgabe bereits zur grundsätzlichen Thematik überleitet. In der Diskussion um die Möglichkeiten und Grenzen, Segnungen und Gefahren der Technologie für den Menschen können die Kursmitglieder durch Einbringen eigener Erfahrungen (z.B. Umgang mit Computer, Internet; Berufspraktika) und Kenntnisse aus anderen Fächern Einiges beisteuern. Eine kontroverse Diskussion der unterschiedlichen Standpunkte lässt sich durch eine Aufteilung des Kurses in zwei Gruppen (pro und contra) in Gang bringen, in der jede Gruppe ihren Standpunkt gegen die andere Gruppe verteidigt. Abschließend – im Plenum oder im Rahmen einer schriftlichen Hausaufgabe – werden die unterschiedlichen Standpunkte mit ihren Argumenten noch einmal gesammelt. Eine abschließende Auswertung kann keine Lösung des Problems anbieten, liefert aber einen Beitrag zur kritischen Bewusstseinsbildung über die Grenzen und Möglichkeiten der Technologie.

Assignments

Pre-reading task

Before you read
p. 18

A lot of science fiction material deals with robots, or other machines which could one day "take over" our world. Try to think of a book or film you have come across where this theme is dealt with, and talk about it. Was it convincing? Frightening? Funny? And how about "progress" along these lines in the real world? What do you know about industrial robots or computers which are "almost human" in one way or another? Most people think that the defeat of Kasparov, the world's best chess player, by a computer, marked a significant step along this road.

Strictly speaking, the Martians described in The War of the Worlds (H.G. Wells, 1898) are not robots, although they seem like robots to the human beings who confront them. This story is the archetype for all later science fiction of this kind. Students will be able to come up with further examples from comics and films.
Industrial computers are capable of performing many repetitive tasks better than human beings, although their range of activities is usually limited. Students will have seen film of robots at work on car production lines (welding, fitting windscreens or facias, spraying on underseal), and should be encouraged to describe the way robots work. Technically-minded students may know something about the role of computers in controlling a robot's movements, and the problems involved in creating, for example, a robot which can do all the things a human hand can do.

Activities

Comments
p. 19

1. In a comment, the writer's opinion matters more than details of the event he is talking about. Try to summarise John Lanchester's view on chess after Kasparov's defeat by writing one sentence for each paragraph of the text.

- Some great chess players have described their game as a sport, even a violent sport.
- Others have added the idea that it is an art.
- In the past we have often seen chess games as artistic and beautiful.
- Kasparov's defeat by a computer makes it clear that chess is only a game.
- Machines are better at this game than we are.
- Fortunately there is no connection between the ability to play chess and other "human" characteristics, such as general intelligence.
- Computers will not go on to achieve consciousness or creativity.
- Deep Blue's victory over Kasparov is still bad news for our species.

2. Do you agree with the statement which forms the title of the article? Write a paragraph giving your own views.

Points which could be made:

Agree
- in a sense there is no point in humans playing chess if computers are better at it
- many players may feel that there isn't much fun in the game any more
- the history of the game as exclusively human history certainly ends here

Disagree
- only a very powerful computer can beat the best human chess players – irrelevant for ordinary players
- small computers actually help humans to play better
- the role of computers is part of the modern history of the game

Work in groups. Make a list of all the areas where machines (including computers) are doing things, or are soon likely to be doing things, which only human beings could do in the past. What have we gained? What have we lost? What are the dangers? Pool your ideas and use them to produce your collective comment, taking disagreements within the group into account.

◀ **Man and machines p. 19**

Examples:
mass production techniques in general, word processors replacing typewriters (perhaps soon letters will be typed direct from the spoken word), industrial robots of all kinds replacing manual workers, cash points replacing cashiers in banks, speaking computers giving advice on timetables, cinema programmes etc., programmed lawnmowers and vacuum cleaners already at the experimental stage.

Gains:
- humans can concentrate on less repetitive work
- lower costs
- efficiency (computers are usually more reliable, and don't take days off)

Losses:
- unemployed manual workers
- less scope for craftsmanship
- less personal contact, de-humanized environment

Additional assignments

1. Make a list of all the items of equipment in and around the home in which a computer or chip of one kind or another can be found (will involve some dictionary work), explain in English what functions the chip performs, and if possible describe how similar equipment functioned in the past without a chip.

e.g. washing machine – operated by means of a simple rotary switch. Now capable of sophisticated chip-controlled programmes at the press of a button.

2. Debate: Do computers and robots destroy jobs – or create them for countries which take the lead in this technology?

A column: *Manhunt* Andrew Billen

Author | Andrew Billen is a respected *Observer* columnist.

About the text | Andrew Billen's brief article, combined with the dramatic photograph of Beachy Head, should appeal to readers because of the good, modern informal style and the potential drama of the situation. We are all – including level-headed policemen – likely to jump to conclusions in a case like this. Most innocent citizens would be worried if they heard the police were looking for them, and also by the fact that in a so-called free country, they could be found so quickly.

Synopsis of the text | The author describes how two policemen were sent out to search for him at his home and at the Observer offices, because he had been reported missing by the Sussex constabulary who had found his car, apparently abandoned, in the car park at Beachy Head, an extremely high cliff on the Sussex coast. Suicide was suspected. He and a friend had in fact walked from their car to a pub where they had stayed the night, and walked back to collect the car the next day. The police had launched a search because Beachy Head is a well-known destination for suicides.

They were very pleased to see that Billen was still alive, but nevertheless made it clear that a lot of public money had been "wasted". After the event the author began wondering about various aspects of the incident. He rang to ask the police why they had carried out an unnecessary search, and how they had found him. The answers were, respectively, the popularity of Beachy Head for suicides, and "old-fashioned detective work."

He was left with a vague feeling of uneasiness, a mixture of returning from the dead, comedy and a hint of a police state.

Unterrichts-empfehlungen | Billens Artikel eignet sich besonders für die vertiefende methodische Schulung des intensiven Lesens. Hier lässt sich beispielhaft verdeutlichen, wie inhaltsbezogene Fragen zum Verständnis des Gedankenganges und Fragen, die auf die Wirkung stilistischer Mittel auf den Leser zielen, den Erschließungsprozess sinnvoll steuern. Somit erfolgt die Arbeit mit diesem Text vornehmlich anhand der Beantwortung der am Rand abgedruckten Fragen. Dies kann in Einzelarbeit bzw. in Partnerarbeit mit einer anschließenden gemeinsamen Auswertung im Plenum geschehen. Die darauf folgende Beschäftigung mit dem Fragenapparat der "Activities" erfolgt in Entsprechung zur Vorarbeit mit einer deutlichen Schwerpunktsetzung auf dem Bereich der *writing techniques*. In einer produktorientierten Phase wird im Anschluss daran eine Umsetzung der hier kennen gelernten Aspekte versucht sowie das Verfassen einer eigenen Kolumne *(Your column)* geprobt. Diese Phase kann im Unterricht eingeleitet und in häuslicher Arbeit weitergeführt werden.

Chapter 1: Newspapers 33

Assignments

Pre-reading task

Work in groups. Look at the photograph of Beachy Head, a massive cliff on the South Coast of England. Collect as many reactions to and thoughts about the photograph as you can. Report your findings to the other groups.

◀ **Before you read ...
p. 20**

Possible reactions:
- enormous height, windy from the top, probably views across to France on a clear day
- fear of heights – not wanting to go too near the edge
- link with the white cliffs of Dover
- boat dwarfed by lighthouse, lighthouse dwarfed by cliff
- cliff somehow threatening because of its height and the sheer drop
- might make even normal people wonder briefly about jumping off
- Importance of the English Channel in British history.

While-reading tasks

Why do you think the author chose the expression "a brace of bobbies"?

◀ **p. 20**

A brace of normally refers to a pair of birds which have been shot by hunters. In connection with the affectionate term bobbies for the police, the effect is humorous.

Why sweet tea?

◀ **p. 20**

Sweet tea is the traditional drink to offer people in any kind of crisis (perhaps plus something a little stronger!).

Why mention the height?

◀ **p. 21**

To emphasise the fact that the cliff is really exceptionally high, and draw the reader's attention to its "suicide potential".

What did the police have reason to believe?

◀ **p. 21**

That the author's car was still in the carpark the next morning because he had committed suicide.

Why mention the helicopter?

◀ **p. 21**

Because it will have cost a lot of money to send a helicopter to look for the author, and perhaps the police want him to feel a little guilty for (unwittingly) causing them so much trouble.

What two meanings of "to hit rock bottom" are referred to here?

◀ **p. 21**

1. to feel very depressed (and in a mood to consider suicide)
2. to actually hit the rocks at the bottom of the cliff.

Interpreting the text
p. 21 - 22

Activities

1. **What assumptions did the writer and his colleagues at work make when they found out the police were looking for him?**

The author's colleagues assumed or pretended to assume that he must have committed some sort of crime.
The author himself assumed that something terrible must have happened to a member of his family.

2. **What assumption did the police make when they found the empty car at Beachy Head? Why?**

They assumed that he had jumped off the cliff and committed suicide because a) his car appeared to have been abandoned, and b) quite a number of people commit suicide at this point every year.

3. **Why mention the problems with builders (start of the third paragraph)?**

Builders in Britain have the reputation of not turning up at the agreed time and then not doing the job properly. People who call in the builders often end up feeling rather desperate. (compare with German attitudes to *Handwerker*)

4. **In what circumstances might a normal person admit to being "half in love with easeful death"?**

Students could mention, for example an unhappy love affair, being permanently in pain, incurably ill, or living on the streets in winter.

5. **Why does the writer refer to "the incensed rate-payer" and "the Conspiracy Theorist Within"?**

These are both potential aspects of his own personality, and also quite commonly-used phrases. The first, for example could appear in place of a signature at the end of a letter to *The Times* protesting about high taxes or ways in which the taxpayer's money is allegedly wasted. A conspiracy theorist would be someone who believes that people are hatching plots all around him (cf. the widely-held belief in the Arab world that Princess Diana's death was not an accident).

6. **How do people the author has told the story to react?**

They feel generally rather uneasy about it because even the suspicion that a friend might have committed suicide is not a pleasant thought. There is an element of comedy in their reactions, and also a sense that we are being watched by some kind of potential "Big Brother".

Writing techniques
p. 22

1. **What steps does the writer take to engage our interest at the beginning?**

Students could mention:
- the title *Manhunt*
- the contrast between the first two sentences
- the threat in the expression *never harbinger joy*

- the questions about the authors "crime"
- the mention of murder

2. At what point in the text does he start to explain what actually happened?

With the sentence, "A friend and I had parked ... "

3. Whereabouts does he start to reflect on the results of his "disappearance"?

Either "So, I realised, was I" or "But when that fleeting euphoria passed ..."

4. Comment briefly on the conclusion. What kinds of material does the writer include? How about the last sentence?

Points that could be made:
- Use of *resonate* – suggests that the story causes "sympathetic vibrations" in readers.
- *resurrection myth* – regligious connotations
- *Keystone Cops* – slapstick black and white film comedy
- *police state* – echoes of communism or 1984.

Last sentence – See the answer to the last *while-reading* task.

5. Why do you think the writer uses both literary and colloquial expressions in his article? Collect some examples of each kind of vocabulary.

Reasons for using both types of expression:
- personal style
- humour
- does not want his column to be taken too seriously
- wants readers to realise that he is well-educated
- wants to share little jokes/understanding of references with them
- contrast
- echoing formal/wordy style used in police reports

literary/formal	colloquial
harbinger	brace of bobbies
Sussex constabulary	coppers
had been issued	I felt *like* I'd been given ...
They thus had reason to believe	cop shop
conceded	piped up
fleeting euphoria	you know
half in love with easeful death	hit rock bottom
incensed	
Conspiracy Theorist within resurrection myth	

A factual report: *Giant gates keep sea at bay* Isabel Conway

About the text

This article from *The European* was chosen as an example of English used for international and technical purposes which have nothing to do with the English-speaking countries. There is so much hard information in it that it is difficult to summarise it without leaving out important facts.
The really dramatic thing about the *Giant Gates*, is that they should be able to hold back the might of the North Sea in a storm, and save Holland from its ancient enemy.

Synopsis of the text

The author begins by reminding readers of previous flood disasters in Holland. In 1953 dykes broke, and the North Sea drowned nearly 2000 people. There was less serious flooding in 1995. A quarter of Holland is below sea level, but 65% of the country would be flooded by the tide every day were it not for the dykes. The Delta project is a milestone in Holland's battle against the sea. A labyrinth of dykes and barriers has been built to protect threatened parts of the coast from the sea.
The Storm Surge Barrier which was opened by Queen Beatrix in 1997, is the last link in the chain. It has been built at the point where the Meuse and Rhine flow into the North Sea.
The plans were made in the aftermath of the 1953 disaster. According to the project manager, the risk of Holland being flooded again is once in 10,000 years. The idea behind the enormous feat of engineering is quite simple. Two huge gates are mounted on a massive balljoint.
When there is a storm warning, the gates, 22m. high and longer than the height of the Eiffel Tower, are closed over a period of two and a half hours. They are designed to resist the worst possible storms. Experts expect the gates to be used once every ten years on average.
Other parts of the delta are protected by giant piers. Special ships were used to move the heavy sections into position. They rest on concrete blocks which themselves rest on a special foundation of sand, heavy stone and gravel.
Computers assess water-levels and weather forecasts, and close the gates automatically when necessary. The Dutch are very proud of the Delta Project, which has been studied by engineering experts from all over the world.

Unterrichts-empfehlungen

Die Arbeit mit diesem Text bietet sich vornehmlich unter dem Aspekt einer produktionsorientierten Zielsetzung an. Die zentrale Stellung der Berichtform in der englischsprachigen Presselandschaft fordert zu einer intensiven Beschäftigung mit den Produktionsstrategien dieser Textform heraus. Es bietet sich an, mit dem Erstellen einer Liste strategischer Mittel für die Komposition eines *factual report* zu beginnen. Hier kann ohne Zweifel auf Vorkenntnisse der Kursmitglieder aus dem Deutschunterricht bzw. eigener Leseerfahrung zurückgegriffen werden. Die gemeinsam erstellte

Liste kann nicht abschließenden Charakter tragen. Sie wird vielmehr im Rahmen der Erschließungsarbeit des Textes ergänzt. Hier zielt insbesondere der Fragenapparat zu *A question of style* auf die Bedeutung einzelner Stilmittel für diesen Texttypus anhand konkreter Beispiele ab. Die Aufgabe, einen eigenen *factual report* zu verfassen, kann im Rahmen einer Hausaufgabe erfolgen. Es sollte jedoch schon bei der Aufgabenstellung deutlich gemacht werden, dass nicht allein die Produktion eines Textes gefragt ist. Vielmehr kann der eigene Text im Rahmen einer extensiven Auswertungsphase vom jeweiligen Kursmitglied zusätzlich in Bezug auf verwendete Stilmittel und Produktionsstrategien erläutert und deren Wirkungsweise im jeweiligen Kontext gemeinsam evaluiert werden. Dieser Weg mag hilfreicher sein, sich der Konstruktionsprinzipien dieser Textform bewusster zu werden.

Assignments

Pre-reading task

... If you were a journalist, how might you try to keep a reader's interest when he or she is reading a factual article you have been asked to write? Make a list of possible strategies ...

◀ **Before you read** p. 22

Possible strategies might include:
- dramatic use of facts and figures
- comparisons which emphasise the special quality of the event or project in question
- links with famous people
- links with past disasters (e.g. mention accidents which happened on an old road now replaced by a motorway)
- emphasise the skills and/or special measures required
- Use emotive language where appropriate

Activities

Write a straightforward description of the Storm Surge Barrier in your own words. Make sure a reader would understand how it works from your description. Use a labelled drawing if you think this would help the reader.

◀ **Facts and figures** p. 24

The Storm Surge Barrier consists of two huge, floating gates, which pivot on a balljoint. They move rather like a human elbow. When there is a storm warning, they are automatically closed, a process which takes two and a half hours. Computers are used to assess water levels and the weather situation, and close the gates automatically when necessary. It is believed that this will make errors less likely.

1. Make a list of emotionally-charged words from the article, and check their meanings. Why did the writer use this kind of language in an article about an engineering project?

◀ **A question of style** p. 24

Emotionally-charged words:
ruptured, shiver of fear, catastrophic, raw power, huge, widespread devastation, vivid, vulnerable, forced to flee, milestone, watery invasion, disastrous, I will sleep easier in my bed, enormous, heaviest conceivable, pounding, immense, old battle against the sea.

Reason for using this kind of vocabulary:
The writer is trying to show readers that an engineering project can be seen as something very exciting in its own right, and also remind them that without it, "excitement" of a very unpleasant kind would be a constant threat in Holland.

2. What role does direct speech play in this article?

It is used as follows:
- to give the first-hand views of the project manager
- both his personal reactions and some details of the engineering are in his words.
- his words are also used to express Dutch pride in the achievement.

You are the reporter p. 24

Write a report on a real event in your own town or part of the country, using a similar range of techniques.

It would be a good idea for the teacher to bring in a local newspaper and point out some suitable items. S/he could also remind students that they should answer the "wh-questions" (what, when, where, who) near the beginning (how and why come later as a rule), and make use of direct speech/comments by experts where appropriate. It is important to make the article interesting, even though in this case it should be mainly factual.

A sports report: *Serene Chang serves the Lord* Kevin Mitchell

About the text

The text is an interesting blend of personal opinions from the two players and comments by the author. It was chosen rather than a straightforward report on a match because there is more to say about it, and it should not go out of date even if one or other of the players slips down the rankings. The very different backgrounds of two players trying to succeed at the same game should make the text interesting for students.

Synopsis of the text

The text compares the very different backgrounds of the tennis players Tim Henman and Michael Chang. Henman is an ex-public schoolboy and Oxford graduate who feels that his comfortable home background and privileged education have given him the confidence to succeed. The author feels that Henman should also acknowledge that the tennis court in his wealthy parents' garden and the services of a top coach have given him a huge start compared with ordinary kids who do not have these advantages. Having "a nice family" is important, but it is only part of the story. Chang's family is also very important, as are his strong religious

convictions. The Changs emigrated from Taiwan to the US in 1948, and struggled to succeed like millions of other immigrant families. Michael Chang and his brother Carl played tennis in threadbare old shoes very different from the brand-new Reeboks Chang wears nowadays. The Chang brothers used rackets and tennis balls until they fell to pieces. Their parents took them to tournaments in a van. They spent their nights in cheap motels. Their mother remembers these times as "a lot of fun."
Henman seems just as dedicated, but he has not been tested on the tennis circuit for as long as Chang. He has not had as many ups and downs, and does not yet possess Chang's "quiet calm." Chang feels that his religion helps him to stand up to the stresses and pressures of world-class tennis. He knows that if you do your best you cannot ask more of yourself, and nor can anyone else.
Henman, for his part, is under tremendous pressure from tennis fans in Britain, who have not had a winner for a long time. Chang thinks that pressure and stress can help people to grow. In fact, he feels that hard times on the court have helped him to mature and grow in character.
It might be easier for Chang to lose.

Unterrichts-empfehlungen

Der Text bietet zahlreiche Ansätze für handlungs- und produktionsorientiertes Arbeiten. Nach der vorbereitenden *Pre-reading task* lässt sich der Text anhand der *while-reading tasks* sowie der Aufgabenstellung unter *The gist* in Einzel- oder Partnerarbeit erschließen und im Anschluss gemeinsam auswerten. Der Aufgabenapparat enthält detaillierte Hinweise für das weitere Vorgehen. Hier bietet sich die Möglichkeit handlungsorientiertes Arbeiten mit dem Üben von Präsentationstechniken zu verbinden. Das Vortragen eines weitgehend vorbereiteten Dialogs im Rahmen einer Talk-Show-Simulation gibt auch zurückhaltenden Kursmitgliedern Gelegenheit zur Übung sprachlicher Flexibilität mit der Zielsetzung, sich zunehmend freier äußern zu können. Es ist angesichts der Kurszusammensetzung zu überlegen, ob das Gespräch durch spontane Fragen ergänzt und ob diese Übung u.U. einmal probeweise auf Video mitgeschnitten wird um eine sorgfältige Analyse nicht nur des fremdsprachlichen Aspekts, sondern auch des Gesprächsverhaltens vorzunehmen. Die anfänglich sicherlich vorhandenen Bedenken lassen sich im Gespräch über den praktischen Nutzen eines solchen Verfahrens (Vorbereitung von Vorstellungsgesprächen als ein Beispiel für den Stellenwert von Präsentationstechniken im Beschäftigungssektor unserer Gesellschaft) ausräumen.

Assignments

Pre-reading task

This article compares the background and attitudes to the game of two well-known tennis players, Henman and Chang. What might some of the differences and similarities be? What ideas do you get when you look at the photos?

◀ **Before you read** p. 25

See the suggestions for the first activity. Comments on the photos could be:
Henman: very English-looking, possibly a bit arrogant, good-looking in a conventional way.
Chang: Ethnically Chinese. Sometimes hard for Westerners to tell what he is thinking, appears mentally strong.

While-reading tasks

p. 25 ▶ Can you explain the word-play in the headline?

A tennis player serves to start the rally (and try to win the point), but while Chang serves the ball (and plays tennis in general) he also feels that he is serving the Lord.

p. 25 ▶ Do you think Henman sounds too confident, even big-headed, or is this kind of confidence necessary in a successful sportsman or woman?

Answer could be along the following lines:
Confidence no doubt helps a sportsman or woman to succeed, but it does not necessarily make him or her a nice person. Henman comes across as someone whose life has been too easy. He seems very compacent about his wealthy background, to the extent that he seems to take his very considerable advantages for granted.

p. 25 ▶ What exactly is the author complaining about here?

The author feels that Henman plays down his financial advantages. Having your own tennis court and a top coach from an early age is rather more than just "a nice family." Plenty of children have nice families – but not very much money, and it's the money that makes the difference.

p. 26 ▶ What does this sentence tell us about the author's attitude to religion?

It tells us that the author doesn't take religion very seriously (although Chang clearly does).

p. 26 ▶ Why might Mrs Chang think this time was "the best fun of all"?

The Changs didn't have much money in those days, but they were all working together for Michael's success, and they had a lot of laughs. Money and fame have brought more stress and pressures. Students could also mention that well-known tennis players get a lot of media attention.

p. 26 ▶ Where would you draw the line between 'pocket money' and 'big bucks'?

Students should be encouraged to take part in an informal debate on this topic. Points which should emerge:
- Huge differences in income between different career groups and between people in rich and poor countries.

- What kind of purchase for the students personally would be something they could buy with their pocket money – and what would they consider as expensive? Try to get them to talk about their personal borderline.
- What senior politicians earn would be pocket money for top footballers and pop stars. How do students feel about this? Do they generally accept the levels of earning for different kinds of jobs?

It's not so easy for Henman either. Why not? ◀ p. 26

As Britain has not had any really successful tennis players for a very long time, there is a feverish atmosphere in his home country every time Henman plays. People desperately want him to win.
(Students may know that Britain has a second successful player, Greg Rusedsky, who was rather more successful than Henman at the time of writing. However, Rusedsky came over to Britain from Canada, and he looks and sounds North American in spite of his British mother, whereas Henman is every inch a Brit.)

How do you feel about this view of pressure and stress? ◀ p. 27

The standard view here is that a certain amount of pressure and stress will encourage people with strong personalities to work harder in their chosen field. However, too much stress can cause unhappiness, nervous complaints, even a breakdown. Not everyone thrives on stress. Some people can only work effectively in a stress-free environment.

Why might this be? ◀ p. 27

Henman has not had many ups and downs yet. His apparently unshakeable confidence might be destroyed by lack of success. Chang's long struggle to succeed in difficult circumstances, plus his deep religious beliefs, would help him to treat a bad patch philosophically.

Activities

Divide a page down the middle and write short parallel profiles of the two players, using subheadings of your own choice. Write a short paragraph at the end summarising the results. ◀ The gist p. 27

What follows is only intended as a suggestion.

HENMAN	CHANG
background	**background**
prosperous, private education, secure member of English middle class, own tennis court at home, coach from an early age.	poverty in the early years, shared struggles of an immigrant family, normal education.
personality	**personality**
confident, prepared to work very hard and do his best, sees himself as a confident person as the result of his upbringing	Also prepared to work hard on court and do his best. At peace with himself. Believes he is using a God-given talent.

career	**career**
relatively short, considerable success early on. Students will be able to add more recent information	more than a decade, near the top of the world rankings most of the time, but has failed to win at the very highest level except for one Paris Open. Has had his ups and downs.
attitude to stress/ lack of success	**attitude to stress/ lack of success**
Not really tested yet, but under tremendous pressure to succeed because Britain is short of good tennis players	Able to cope well in adverse circumstances because of his early struggles, his religious beliefs and his long experience of the game. Believes that stress and pressure have helped him to mature.

Summary

Henman and Chang both have very supportive families, although there were big social and financial differences in the way they were brought up. Both men are prepared to work very hard on and off court, and both are very determined to succeed. Henman has not so far come up against serious difficulties. Chang's tougher background, greater experience and religious beliefs may help him to cope better when times are hard.

A chat show ▶ p. 27

Work in threes. Write and practise a dialogue in which a chat show host talks to Henman and Chang, trying to bring out the differences between them, provoke them a bit, have a bit of fun at their expense, etc.

If students have worked through the activity above they should have no problems with this assignment.

Your attitude to sport ▶ p. 27

Ask your partner to interview you about your attitude to sport. He or she should try to find out if you participate actively, play regularly for a club, do sports seriously or just for fun or to keep fit, whether you follow sports on TV and in the newspapers, if you have sporting heroes/heroines etc.

Plenty of ideas for questions above. Answers are personal.

Self-analysis ▶ p. 27

Could you get to the top in sport or in some other field? Are you good at coping with stress and pressures? How ambitious are you? Does religion play a role in your life? Write roughly a page about your own aspirations, and your chances of realising them.

Students should make use of expressions such as On the whole, as a rule, I think I'm the kind of person who ..., I'm not (very) ambitious in some ways, but ..., I've always been very interested in ..., I don't mind if (I only get average grades)

Additional Text: Advertisement

Photographer: Nick Knight

Activities

1. Describe what you can see in the illustrations
2. How do the illustrations link up with the text in large print?
3. Do you know anything about the kind of image Volvo cars had a few years ago, in Britain and elsewhere.
4. What do you think Volvo are trying to achieve with this advertisement?
5. Read the text. Why do you think:
   - that the reader/purchaser is praised and addressed personally in this way?
   - the powerful engine is referred to as "pure coincidence"?
   - an Italian motoring magazine is quoted when it comes to the appearance of the car?
6. Do you think this is a successful advertisement? Is it honest? What about the psychology behind it? Write a brief assessment.

Solutions

1. The car is in central position, looking fairly low and sporty, although it is an estate car (*Kombi*). It has expensive-looking alloy wheels. On the left we can see a happy child sitting on what looks like a built-in child

safety seat. The ropes and strong metal clips seem to be climbing equipment. On the right we can see a running shoe, presumably with a foot inside it. The position of the shoe suggests someone actually running.

2. The text in large print mentions both safety and power/potential high speed. The illustrations on the left – which the eye naturally falls on first – link up with safety. Parents would like to feel that their (vulnerable) children are safe in the car. Climbing equipment has to be strong enough to support the climber's weight, and completely reliable. The running shoe on the right links up with power and speed.

3. In the past Volvos were believed to be very solidly-built and safe, with plenty of room for sports gear, holiday luggage etc., but not very exciting. One motoring magazine gave as both the main advantage and disadvantage of older Volvos "Built like a tank". English *Landeskunde*: Volvos have been seen in the past as a kind of on-road Land/Range-Rover kind of car with a fairly upper class image, associated with the "green wellie brigade" (wellie = wellington boot = *Gummistiefel*) – tweed-wearing country people).

4. They want to keep the safety image, but add sporting, high performance elements in order to appeal to a younger, wealthy, performance-orientated group of customers without losing their traditional market.

5. - The intention is to flatter the reader and feed his ego by using words like *wisely*
   - Old and new Volvo drivers may well have a bad conscience about buying such a powerful car nowadays – but they will enjoy the performance and prestige. Of course it is not "pure coincidence" at all that Volvo have decided to make this car so powerful. They know that this kind of car is generally purchased by a man, that cars are associated with male potency, and that men like to tell other men how powerful their cars are.
   - The Italians are seen as leaders in smart, sexy design, both in clothes and cars. Volvo are probably hoping their cars will be associated with Versace, Gucci, Ferrari, etc.

6. The advertisement will probably be successful in helping to change Volvo's image. Turbos, and a lot of horsepower combined with safety and attractive design amount to a very persuasive package. Safety, strength and high performance will definitely appeal to potential male purchasers, particularly as the high performance is played down (but mentioned in large print and backed up by the statistics in the small print). From a psychological point of view, this approach is intended to make the purchaser feel better about buying a high-performance car in an environmentally-conscious era. Words such as *practical rational*, *wisely* reinforce the message that is not irresponsible to buy this kind of car. We can assume that buyers of more traditional Volvos were not very interested in high performance, and many of them will have been environmentalists. Volvo has attempted to keep traditional customers on board while appealing at the same time to a younger, more fashion and performance-orientated clientele. The advertisement is clever, but questionable on ethical grounds.

Chapter 2: Television

Vorbemerkungen zum Kapitel

Für den Einsatz im Kursunterricht gilt Ähnliches wie für das erste Kapitel. Die Reihenfolge der Bearbeitung der einzelnen Texte bzw. Videosequenzen hängt von der jeweiligen unterrichtlichen Schwerpunktsetzung ab. Es empfiehlt sich jedoch, alle Programmformen vorzustellen und zu besprechen um den Schülerinnen und Schülern einen ausreichenden Überblick über das englische Fernsehen zu geben. Falls die Video- und Fernsehaufzeichnungen nicht zur Verfügung stehen, muss mit den im Buch abgedruckten Transkriptionen gearbeitet werden. Für die Arbeit mit den Videosequenzen können folgende Empfehlungen gegeben werden:

- Der Einsatz von Videosequenzen, d.h. Auszügen aus einem Film, einer Fernsehserie, etc. bedarf einer unmittelbaren inhaltlichen Anbindung an das Unterrichtsthema. Das kann z.B. in einem Rahmen wie dem hier vorgestellten geschehen. Die in diesem Heft abgedruckten Transkriptionen können darüber hinaus auch in einem anderen thematischen Zusammenhang Gegenstand des Unterrichts sein. Entsprechend wird auf eine solche Einsatzmöglichkeit im Rahmen der jeweiligen Unterrichtsempfehlungen verwiesen.
- Die Video- oder Filmsequenz ist Gegenstand intensiver unterrichtlicher Beschäftigung. Aus diesem Grunde ist es nahe liegend, den zeitlichen Umfang eines Auszugs so zu begrenzen, dass Kursteilnehmer sinnvoll damit arbeiten können. Eine Länge von etwa 5 Minuten erscheint angemessen. Eine komplette Sequenz aus *Fawlty Towers* oder *Yes, Prime Minister* kann mit einem Kurs erst nach gezielter Vorarbeit und detaillierten Einzelanalysen zu Teilen einer Sequenz sinnvoll als Ganzes eingesetzt werden, ohne Schüler durch die Fülle sprachlicher, inhaltlicher und bildlicher Informationen zu überfordern und zu viele Fragen offen zu lassen.
- Die Arbeit mit Video und Film eröffnet die Möglichkeit zu unterschiedlichen Arbeits- und Sozialformen im Unterricht, wie z.B. arbeitsteiliger Gruppenarbeit mit unterschiedlichen Beobachtungsaufgaben. Die Ergebnisse einzelner Gruppe können dem Kurs präsentiert werden und sind Gegenstand von Diskussionen.
- Beobachtungsaufgaben schließen ein: Arbeitsaufträge zur Informationsverarbeitung (z.B. einfache und komplexe Erkennungsaufgaben; die Arbeit mit Lückentexten, die nur einen Teil des Videotextes wiedergeben; Checklisten und standardisierte Fragebögen – etwa bei der Besprechung von Werbespots, Nachrichtensendungen oder gattungsbezogenen Videosequenzen – z.B. *What makes a good comedy?*), Übungen zur Sprachproduktion und -reproduktion (Wiederholen zur Schulung von Aussprache, Betonung und Intonation; Erinnern ganzer oder einzelner Teile bestimmter Äußerungen; die Arbeit mit deutschen Untertiteln mit dem Ziel, das englische Original – bei abgeschaltetem Ton – zu erarbeiten; Formen szenischer Darstellung) und zur Interaktion (Bild ohne Ton; Ton ohne Bild

mit Hypothesenbildungen; Profilerstellung einzelner Figuren; Rollenspiel – Stoppen einer Sequenz und Fortführung des Dialogs im Kurs; kulturübergreifende Vergleiche).

Im Einzelnen sind zu den unterschiedlichen Auszügen Empfehlungen in Bezug auf mögliche Formen des unterrichtlichen Einsatzes gemacht worden, die im Prinzip auch für den Umgang mit (den) anderen Auszügen mit bzw. ohne Transkription anwendbar sind. Allerdings wird im Sinne des Methodenwechsels und des Motivationserhalts empfohlen, keine schematische Anwendung der Übungsformen im Sinne einer starren Reihenfolge, die für jeden Text gut ist, vorzunehmen. Stattdessen sollte jede Transkription bzw. Videosequenz vor dem Hintergrund der sprachlichen Möglichkeiten der Lerngruppe, der inhaltlichen Einbettung in eine Unterrichtsreihe, sowie deren fremdsprachliche wie methodische Ziele geprüft und unterrichtsmethodisch aufgearbeitet werden.

Bezugsadressen für die Videos
- The Old Bookshop, Güldener Trog 5, 59423 Unna, Tel. 0 23 03 / 2 34 64, Fax 0 23 03 / 2 35 63
- Mail-Order-Kaiser, 80791 München, Tel. 0 89 / 3 60 82 - 2 12, Fax 0 89 / 3 60 82 - 2 40, E-Mail: kaiser@mail-order-kaiser.de, Internet: http://www.mail-order-kaiser.de

Start here

About the text	The text is intended to give brief factual information about British television.
Synopsis of the text	The BBC began broadcasting in 1932 but television did not make much impact until 1953 (coronation of Queen Elizabeth 2). Two years later saw the start of ITV. The 1960's saw the introduction of second channels for both authorities, and of colour television. More recently satellite TV has become popular, but cable TV plays a very minor role in Britain at present. ITV (27% of viewers) and BBC1 (21%) remain by the far the most popular choices.
Unterrichtsempfehlungen zu den Einstiegsmaterialien auf S. 29 - 31	Der Einstieg in diesen Teil des Heftes kann über eine Art *brainstorming* zum Thema der *personal viewing habits* (darauf wird mit der Aufgabe auf S. 30: *What's on TV this evening?* hingearbeitet) und einer anschließenden zumindest groben Systematisierung erfolgen. Dazu und auch der Möglichkeit des späteren Rückgriffs wegen – s.u. – sollten die Ergebnisse dieser Phase auf einer Folie, nicht auf der Tafel festgehalten werden. Wenngleich die individuelle Schwerpunktsetzung hier exakt nicht vorweggenommen werden kann, lassen sich bestimmte Richtungen, die die persönliche Programm- und Themenauswahl der Kursmitglieder beim Fernsehkonsum zum Ausdruck bringen, durchaus als wahrscheinlich prognostizieren: Vorliebe für Musiksender: MTV, Viva, Onyx usw. Je nach inhaltlicher Schwerpunkt-

setzung der Reihe lässt sich nach Erarbeitung eines Kriterienkatalogs zur Betrachtung dieser Spots das eine oder andere Beispiel besprechen.
- ■ Fernsehen als Informationsquelle: Nachrichtensendungen unterschiedlicher Art gehören sicherlich zum Repertoire einiger Schüler und Schülerinnen. Eine Reihe britischer und amerikanischer Nachrichtensender sind in Deutschland unverschlüsselt über Satellit und teilweise über Kabel zu empfangen. Hier liegt langfristig eine große Chance für die Arbeit eines jeden Grund- und vor allem Leistungskurses: das Fernsehen bringt die englische Sprache direkt ins Haus bzw. ins Klassenzimmer. Es ist naheliegend, diesen ersten direk-ten Kontakt mit solchen Programmen (Sky News, CNN, Channel 5, CNBC, NBC Superchannel) für den Unterricht mit einiger Regelmäßigkeit zu nutzen, wann immer sich inhaltlich die Möglichkeit zum Einsatz eröffnet. Damit kann – von der Sachinformation einmal abgesehen – vor allem die sprachliche Schulung einer Lerngruppe profitieren. Die Gewöhnung an authentisches Englisch in unterschiedlichen Varianten ist ebenso erforderlich wie eine breite Schulung des Hörverständnisses.
- ■ Die Vorlieben mancher Schüler und Schülerinnen für Filme und Fernsehserien mag ihnen die Dominanz dieser Produktionen aus den USA und GB sowie anderen englischsprachigen Ländern verdeutlichen. Warum daher nicht auch mal eine Folge einer solchen Reihe in englischer Sprache (z.B. *X-Files*, *Star Trek*, oder aus dem Comics-/Cartoonbereich *The Simpsons*)?

Wenn der zeitliche Rahmen ausreicht und die langfristigen inhaltlichen und sprachlichen Zielsetzungen der Kursarbeit es als erstrebenswert erscheinen lassen, sind hier Möglichkeiten zu einer langfristigen Planung und Organisation gegeben: Kursmitglieder, die über die entsprechenden Anlagen zu Hause verfügen, können Sendungen auswählen und auf Band aufnehmen um sie zu einem geeigneten Zeitpunkt im Kurs zu besprechen. Dabei sollte die Kursleitung deutlich machen, dass die auswählenden Gruppen sich auf einen oder zwei Auszüge aus einer Nachrichtensendung, ein oder zwei englischsprachige Videospots, einen Auszug aus einem Comic oder Film/Serie aus britischer Produktion beschränken sollen, damit diese auch sinnvoll besprochen werden können. So lässt sich neben dem Text ein erster Eindruck vom Fernsehen in englischer Sprache gewinnen.

Der Text auf Seite 29 dient in erster Linie der Hintergrundinformation und kann durch eine Kleingruppe vorbereitet werden, die für die Präsentation des Inhalts vor dem Kurs auch eine Folie für den OHP zur übersichtlichen Veranschaulichung bereithält. Aufgrund der häufigen Veränderungen auf dem Mediensektor ist durchaus zu erwarten, dass einzelne Kursmitglieder aus unterschiedlichen Quellen über neue Fernsehkanäle etwa von *Sky* erfahren haben oder auch über relevante Ergänzungen im Kabelfernsehen und in deutschen Kanälen ausgestrahlte englischsprachige Filme im Zweikanalton Bescheid wissen.

Britain's favourite leisure 'activity' ▶
p. 29

Read the following text about British TV and try to find out the main differences between British and German television and viewing habits.

Points that could be made:
Earlier spread of TV after WW2 in Britain.
BBC2 for culture and special interests rather than with a regional bias, as with German *3. Programme.*
No commerials on BBC programmes, but there are commercials on the public service channels in Germany.
Minor role played by cable TV in Britain.

What's on TV this evening?

About the text

This is a fairly typical evening's viewing. The daytime programmes have been omitted to save space. Note the use of the 12-hour clock. There is no need for learners to understand every word of the fairly difficult text. They should be encouraged to concentrate on programmes they think they might be interested in, and try to work out what they might be about with the help of the notes.

Unterrichts-empfehlungen

In Fortsetzung der im Rahmen des *brainstorming* festgehaltenen Vorlieben zum Fernsehkonsum kann der Aufgabenkomplex *What's on TV this evening?* angegangen werden. Die Programmübersicht kann statt im Unterricht auch in häuslicher Vorbereitung mit den Aufgabenaufträgen der Seite 32 erarbeitet und in der kommenden Stunde dem Kurs in Form individueller Beiträge präsentiert werden.

Assignments

Pre-reading task

Before you read ... ▶
p. 30

Work in groups. Do you watch more or less TV than your classmates? More or less than your parents? Why do you think this is? Are there any programmes you try never to miss – or would never dream of watching? Do you have any major complaints about German TV? Would you expect things to be any different in Britain? Prepare a brief report which you can read out to the class.

Mainly personal opinions. It would help pupils if they were give some typical programme categories, e.g.
soap opera, news and current affairs, documentary, travel, music programme, nature/animal programme, situational comedy (sitcom), sports, drama, cartoons, nature programme, educational programme, detective/police series, film (action, romantic, spy, comedy, police or detective).

Activities

Without talking to your partner, plan your evening's British television viewing on the basis of the programmes on the previous pages (we'll assume you have nothing better to do in the evening). Talk to one another about your choices, and try to reach agreement on what you would watch. Is a compromise possible, or would you need two TV sets?

◀ **A question of choice** p. 32

Learners should be supplied with some gambits for arguments, e.g.

That's all very well, but ...	I'm not the slightest bit
Well, OK, but ...	interested in ...
Yes, but on the other hand ...	Here's my idea for a compromise.
Wouldn't you say that ...	How can you possibly want to watch such rubbish!

1. Try to classify as many of the programmes as possible on the basis of your own list of categories.

◀ **Classifying and comparing** p. 32

For a list of categories, see the pre-reading task above. In most cases the type of programme is clear from the title or the notes.
e.g. Songs of Praise   Music programme
      Oh Doctor Beeching   Sitcom
      The Antiques Inspectors Documentary
      Full Circle   Travel Programme

2. Now choose a typical evening's TV programmes on German television and classify them according to the same list. Are there any important differences?

Progammes in the two countries are basically quite similar. Differences which could emerge:
- More comedy on British TV
- More "culture" and catering for minority interests on BBC2 and Channel 4 (but cf. Arte in Germany)
- American films with the original sound-track.
- More nostalgic programmes on British TV

Now plan your personal perfect evening's view and read it out to the class. You don't have to take this task too seriously.

◀ **In an ideal world ...** p. 32

Teachers should insist that all programme names are in English. Fictional programme names should have an authentic ring to them. Students should be prepared to explain what "their" programmes would be about.

Additional assignment

Work with a partner. Imagine that one of you is an English or American friend who is staying with you. He or she understands some German. Go through the German TV programmes for the coming evening and talk about them. The "English" friend points to things s/he thinks might be interesting. S/he asks you what these programmes are likely to be about, and whether they would be difficult to understand.

Classic comedy: *Fawlty Towers: The Psychiatrist*

Author

The scripts for Fawlty Towers were written by John Cleese, the well-known comic actor, and the actress Connie Booth, who appears in the extract, and was at one time John Cleese's wife.

About the text

The comedy arises from Basil's exaggerated reactions to two different kinds of guests, Mr Johnson, whom he thoroughly disapproves of, and the two doctors, to whom he kow-tows because of their titles. In the process he reveals his own prejudiced and inhibited views, which are not shared by his wife. Learners who are able to view the video should be able to hear the differences in class and accent between the different speakers: Basil and the doctors: so-called received pronunciation, or what most normal English people call a "posh accent". Mr Johnson, and to some extent Sybil, a lower-class London accent.

Synopsis of the text

The extract begins with Sybil chatting to Mr Johnson, a wealthy playboy type with a cockney accent. Sybil finds Mr Johnson attractive, and enjoys his jokes, but Basil is offended by his casual style of dress, in particular the charms he wears round his neck. Basil also regards Mr Johnson as lower class and lacking in intelligence. Sybil suggests that Basil would prefer earlier upper-class role-models, and Basil agrees that at least such men had a certain amount of dignity. Sybil feels that "Mediterranean types" – or even monkeys – at least know how to enjoy themselves.
At this point Dr. Abbott and his wife, also a doctor, enter the hotel, and catch Basil doing a monkey impression. Basil pays little attention to the new guests until he hears the magic word doctor, when he immediately switches to exaggerated politeness. However, he is unable at first (for sexist reasons) to grasp that both husband and wife are doctors.

Unterrichtsempfehlungen

Es bieten sich unterschiedliche Möglichkeiten des Einstiegs zur Erschließung dieses Textes.
1. Einmal kann man mit der grundsätzlichen Frage, was eine gute Komödie ausmacht, einsteigen. Die Kursmitglieder sammeln auf der Grundlage ihrer Fernseh- und Videoerfahrung ebenso wie ihres literarischen Vorwissens Aspekte, die sie als wesentlich für das Gelingen einer Komödie und ihren Erfolg beim Publikum halten. Auch hier lässt sich das Ergebnis auf einer Folie festhalten, wenn im Anschluss an die später erfolgende Lektüre der Transkription und dem gemeinsamen Betrachten des Videoauszugs die neu gewonnenen Erkenntnisse mit den Einstiegsergebnissen und Erwartungen verglichen werden. Als zweiter oder alternativ erster Schritt bietet sich die *pre-reading task* zu John Cleese an.
2. Ebenso ließe sich das Grundgerüst der Fernsehserie vorstellen (vgl. Vorspann zum Text auf S. 32) und gegebenfalls erweitern, wobei Kenntnisse der Kursmitglieder – die Serie ist ja auch in

Deutschland mehrfach gezeigt worden – einbezogen werden können. Die Serie ist in Großbritannien so populär, dass einzelne Äußerungen in den englischen Sprachgebrauch eingegangen sind: Dazu gehören etwa *He's from Barcelona*, eine Referenz an den spanischen Kellner Manuel, sowie Basils hilflose Entschuldigung *I'm just checking the walls*. U.U. ist auch das Ergebnis des *brainstorming* zu den Grundelementen einer gelungenen Komödie hilfreich, da mit Sicherheit dort Einzelelemente, die auch in *Fawlty Towers* zu finden sind, bereits identifiziert wurden. In diesen Zusammenhang gehört auch die Möglichkeit über eventuelle Themen zu sprechen, die sich aus der Situierung der Serie in einem kleinen Hotel, der Kenntnis der Hauptcharaktere, etc. ergeben könnten. Verwiesen sei in diesem Kontext auf Themen wie gesellschaftliche Unterschiede (*The Psychiatrist*; *A Touch of Class*), stereotype Erwartungen und Haltungen gegenüber Ausländern (die Figur von Manuel, dem spanischen Kellner im Hotel, der in jeder Folge Opfer von Basil Fawltys Frustrationen ist) und den Deutschen und ihrer Rolle im Zweiten Weltkrieg gegenüber (in der Folge *The Germans*), den Amerikanern und ihrem forschen, fordernden und Probleme sofort lösen wollenden Auftreten (in der Folge *Waldorf Salad*). Diese Filmsequenzen lassen sich zu unterschiedlichen thematischen Aspekten in Unterrichtsreihen einbauen (z.B. im Zusammenhang des Themenkomplexes *human aggression, British views on Germany*).

3. Die Erarbeitung des Textauszugs selbst kann zunächst durch Lesen in Form einer rein kognitiven Erfassung vorgenommen werden, in deren Verlauf die unterschiedlichen *while-reading tasks* bearbeitet werden. Die Zurückstellung des Videoauszugs soll erreichen, dass im Rahmen eines Gesprächs zunächst über die Umsetzung des Skripts in eine Filmversion gesprochen werden kann. Was bringt den Betrachter zum Lachen? Solche Anlässe sind nicht allein durch den Text vorgegeben, sondern ergeben sich erst bei einer szenischen Umsetzung. (Sollte der Textauszug nicht als Videosequenz vorhanden sein, kann im Anschluss an die hier besprochene Unterrichtsphase der Versuch einer eigenen Inszenierung erfolgen. Ein wesentliche Rolle spielt dabei der in jeder Hinsicht erforderliche Begründungszusammenhang, den der Kurs bei einer entsprechenden Umsetzung liefern muss. Hier geht es um die Grundfrage, warum eine bestimmte Szene, ein bestimmter Dialog so und nicht anders gespielt werden soll.) Ein solcher Textzugang verdeutlicht sehr schnell, dass der Text erst durch zusätzliche Elemente wie etwa Mimik, Gestik, Art der Intonation, Platzierung der Schauspieler usw. Komik entstehen lässt. Es mag helfen, wenn die Diskussion hier weniger ergiebig erscheint, als erwartet werden darf, den Videoauszug einmal ohne Bild und nur mit dem Ton vorzustellen, um gemeinsam zu erfragen, warum an dieser und jener Stelle gelacht wird. Dann kann im Anschluss daran – je nach Möglichkeiten in der Gruppe – der Versuch einer szenischen Erläuterung einzelner Gesprächsteile unternommen werden, bevor der Auszug ganz gesehen wird. Das Vorspielen des Videobandes sollte von entsprechenden Betrachtungsaufträgen für verschiedene Gruppen begleitet werden, die sich auf die einzelnen Figuren, ihrer Gestik, Mimik, Stimmla-

ge, etc., konzentrieren. Nach dem gemeinsamen Besprechen dieser Eindrücke ist Raum für die *Activities* 1 bis 3 auf Seite 35 und die beiden Aufgaben zu *Discussing views*. Hier können im Rahmen der zweiten Aufgabenstellung eine gemeinsame Rückschau betrieben werden und die Ergebnisse der einzelnen Besprechungsschritte zusammengetragen werden. Die Aufgabe *Writing a scene* bezieht sich auf die Sequenz *A Touch of Class*, in der eine ähnliche Situation wie die hier skizzierte Basil in größte Verlegenheit bringt. Der Kurs kann diese Aufgabe als Hausaufgabe vorbereiten und individuell in der kommenden Stunde präsentieren. Für den Fall, dass die Kursleitung Zugang zu dieser Videosequenz hat, besteht im Anschluss an die Besprechung die Gelegenheit für den Kurs, ihre Ergebnisse mit dem Original zu vergleichen.

Assignments

Pre-reading task

Before you watch or read ... p. 32

John Cleese has appeared in a number of television series and films, some of which have been shown in Germany. Can you remember any of them? If you can, describe a scene which has stuck in your memory. What kind of character does John Cleese usually play? Is he in some way "typically British"?

e.g. Monty Python's Flying Circus
Life of Brian
A Fish called Wanda
Fierce Creatures
John Cleese often plays a character close to the stereotyped idea of the English gentleman (well-spoken, restrained emotions, tall and elegant, traditional attitudes), but there is usually panic just under the surface.

While-reading tasks

p. 32

Accents are still very important in England. Try to characterise Mr Johnsons's accent, and compare it with that of Dr Abbot when he appears.

Mr Johnson has a London accent (a mild form of cockney), but he has absolutely no inferiority complex about the way he speaks. Dr. Abbott speaks in an educated way with correct grammar and clear pronunciation. He has a slight posh accent.

p. 33

Basil and Sybil are constantly at war with one another. What do you think Basil's remark "Twice can be arranged" is intended to imply?

He means that it would be possible (for him) to become single again by divorcing, or more likely murdering his wife.

p. 33

How affectionate do you think "my dear" is in English? Can you think of similar expressions in German?

The expression *my dear* is so common that it has lost most of its affectionate meaning. Even *darling* is going the same way. Similar expressions in German would be *Schatz* or *Liebling*.

Chapter 2: Television   53

Do you see the joke here? Why doesn't Basil laugh? ◀ p. 33

The joke is that the use of a French word in an English sentence is pretentious. Basil doesn't laugh because he has no intention of finding anything Mr Johnson says amusing, and because he is annoyed that Sybil finds him entertaining.

Why do you think Basil says this? (ie. Well, that must come in handy.) ◀ p. 33

He assumes that Mr Johnson must have a very active sex life, something Basil disapproves of, so he might find a fertility symbol useful.

What kind of forehead "goes back to the dawn of civilization"? ◀ p. 33

A very low forehead (which does not look as if there is much space for a large brain behind it)

How does Sybil gain a point here in connection with medals? ◀ p. 34

She reminds Basil that people like Earl Haig were not at all averse to wearing medals, even if they weren't on a chain round their necks.

Why do you think Basil freezes? ◀ p. 34

He has just heard the magic word *doctor* – a title for which he automatically feels the greatest respect. He realises that he has not been behaving appropriately in the presence of a doctor so far.

Compare Basil's reaction to the doctor with his reaction to Mr Johnson. ◀ p. 34

Reaction to doctor: automatic respect, politeness, consideration. Reaction to Mr Johnson: looks down on him, refuses to be amused, makes fun of his style of dress, questions his intelligence.

Why can't Basil grasp the fact that Mrs Abbot is a doctor, too? ◀ p. 34

Basil is old-fashioned and unemancipated. In his world only men are doctors (unlike German, English does not have separate words for male and female doctors).

Activities

1. Imagine that you are a psychiatrist. You have watched this scene, and are asked what you think of Basil's behaviour. Write a short report. ◀ The character of Basil Fawlty p. 35

Points which could be made:
- reactions very extreme
- cannot accept people different from himself
- not happily married
- no sense of humour
- ultra-traditional
- exaggerated respect for people perceived as higher up the social scale than himself.
- Probably in need of treatment for insecurity, inability to express his emotions.

2. Why is Basil so annoyed when his wife laughs at Mr Johnson's joke and seems to find him attractive generally?

He is probably a bit jealous – does not like his wife being amused by another man. He refuses point-blank to find Mr Johnson and/or his conversation amusing anyway.

3. What role do you think people like Gladstone, Haig and Baden-Powell might play in Basil's scheme of things?

These were all typical leading Victorian and/or British Empire figures regarded as upright, respectable gentlemen (although Haig's reputation has suffered as a result of his inflexible, unimaginative strategy in the First World War) We can safely assume that Basil admires them as representatives of an older, in his view better Britain.

Discussion views
p. 35

1. "We should not laugh at a man who is a mass of prejudices and clearly in need of psychiatric treatment." How far do you agree with this view of Basil Fawlty?

Points which could be made:
- Only a character played by John Cleese, not the man himself (although Cleese has had psychiatric treatment).
- Basil's behaviour is so exaggerated that we can't take it seriously.
- Many people, ourselves probably included, have prejudices of various kinds. To some extent we may be laughing at ourselves, and this is good for us.

2. "It is no good just reading the script of a comedy programme. The effect depends just as much on what you *see* as what you *hear*." Describe some of the action/body language etc. which occurs during this scene and explain how it contributes to the comedy.

Examples:
Basil staring at Johnson (apparently finds it hard to believe that J. is a member of the same species).
Sybil's body language shows that she is attracted to Johnson.
Basil freezing when he hears the word doctor (realises that this is a special guest requiring special attention and that he should not go in for any more silly antics).
Note Basil's respectful pose in the last screenshot.

A police series: *The Bill*

About the text

The story is rather complicated, but logically constructed, and made interesting by the rivalry between the two sergeants, representing the uniformed police on one side and the CID on the other. An apparently simple case of assault with jealousy as the motive (Chris is sleeping with Leo's wife) gradually turns out to be more sinister. Chris has been trying to make money by working for a drugs dealer, from whom he steals some heroin to sell on his own account. Leo, an honest but quick-tempered character, wants to give the drugs back and end Jill's involvement with Grey, a dangerous criminal. The uniformed police unravel the case and arrive in time to arrest the villains and avoid serious injury to Leo.

The instalment begins when the police are called to a small terraced house by a neighbour. He says it sounded as if someone was being killed. Sgt. Boyden and his men go in and find Chris Darrow lying on the floor, injured. Chris says he was attacked by Leo Morrison. Chris is sleeping with Leo's wife, but everyone thought Leo was in working in Spain.
When Sgt. Beech of the CID finds out about the case, he decides that he will try to find Leo first. There is some rivalry between the two sergeants. An informer, Tommy Wood, tells Sgt. Beech where to find Jill Morrison, and he goes round to her flat. Jill does not know Leo is back. She has told Leo about her affair with Chris, and wants nothing more to do with him.
Meanwhile Sgt. Boyden's team have found Leo in a shopping centre, talking to Tommy Wood. They try to arrest him, but he gets away. They arrest Tommy Wood, who protests noisily and says he wants to see Sgt. Beech.
Back at the station the two sergeants argue about the way each of them is pursuing the case, and Sgt. Beech bets Sgt. Boyden £50 that the CID will have caught Leo by the evening.
Tommy and another friend of Leo's tell Sgt. Beech that Chris is working for a drugs dealer called Tony Grey. Jill is probably involved as well, and Tony Grey seems to be looking for her.
Sgt. Boyden receives a call from a wine bar. Jill Morrison has been threatened by a tall man who fits the description of Tony Grey. She explains that she wanted to talk to Tony before he meets Leo. Leo, who hates drugs, wants to give back a package which Jill and Chris were hoping to sell. Leo does not know that Chris stole the drugs from Tony Grey, who is in a very dangerous mood. The meeting between Tony and Leo is about to take place in Jill's flat. Sgt. Boyden and his team arrive just in time to prevent Leo from being beaten up by Tony Grey and an accomplice. Tony Grey is caught red-handed with the drugs. Leo is arrested for injuring Chris.
In the final scene Sgt. Beech has to pay £50 to Sgt. Boyden. The uniformed police have beaten the CID, who have made no significant progress on the case.

Synopsis of the text

Die *pre-reading task* ist als unmittelbarer Einstieg in die Erarbeitung dieses Textes hilfreich. Die sicherlich breite Fernseh- und Kinoerfahrung der Kursmitglieder kann zu einer beträchtlichen Sammlung an Ergebnissen und Impressionen beitragen. Zu überlegen ist, ob einzelne Ergebnisse dieser Phase zum Zwecke einer abschließenden Auswertung nach Bearbeitung von Text und Videosequenz festgehalten werden sollen. Die sprachliche und inhaltliche Vorbereitung des Textauszugs sollte den Schülerinnen und Schülern aufgrund der Länge als Hausaufgabe rechtzeitig aufgegeben und ein entsprechender Zeitrahmen zur Verfügung gestellt werden. Die häusliche Vorbereitung sollte in Verbindung

Unterrichts- empfehlungen

mit den drei Aufgaben auf Seite 42 erfolgen. Dabei erscheint eine Aufteilung des Kurses in drei Gruppen sinnvoll, sodass sich jeweils ein Drittel der Gruppe um eine Aufgabe kümmert und für die Präsentation im Kurs ihr Material auf Folie bereithält (Zitatensammlung, Notizen, Wortlisten). Damit geht die Darbietung der Besprechung der Hausaufgaben in eine gezielte Diskussion der Fragen im Kursverband über, an der alle Teilnehmer partizipieren können, da das erforderliche Diskussionsmaterial per Folie jedem zugänglich ist. Bei Vorhandensein der Videoaufzeichnung wird nun die filmische Version vorgestellt. Beim zweiten Vorspielen lassen sich auch die *while-viewing tasks* angehen, für deren Beantwortung das Band gestoppt werden kann. Ebenso ist jetzt der Zeitpunkt für die Bearbeitung der sprachbezogenen Aufgaben (S. 43; 1 bis 3) gekommen, die sich ohne Video nicht lösen lassen. Die Erschließung der *characters* als möglicher zusätzlicher Erarbeitungsaspekt bedarf ebenfalls der Videovorlage, da Gestik, Mimik, Intonation etc. wesentliche Informationen liefern, die der Transkription fehlen.

Die beiden weiteren Aufgaben des Apparats sind produktionsorientiert und runden die bislang schwerpunktmäßig textanalytisch ausgerichtete Beschäftigung mit *The Bill* auf einer anderen Ebene sinnvoll ab. Wie ausgiebig hier Aufgabe 2 erarbeitet werden kann, wird nicht nur vom Interesse der Kursteilnehmer und der technischen Ausstattung abhängen, sondern auch von Überlegungen zur Unterrichtsökonomie. Daher ist u.U. an eine Auslagerung in ein Projekt zu denken, das je nach institutioneller Bedingung unterschiedlich platzierbar ist (z.B. als zusätzliche Hausarbeit; als Facharbeit mit entsprechend erweiterter Aufgabenstellung; im Zusammenhang einer fachübergreifenden AG).

Assignments

Pre-reading task

Before you watch or read ... p. 35

Make a list of all the famous detectives you can think of. Which countries are they from? Try to include some great names from the past. Do you have any special favourites or pet hates? Talk about your list with your partner. Give reasons for your choices. Describe a scene which you found particularly gripping. Why do you think police and detective series have remained so popular?

Famous detectives:
e.g. Sherlock Holmes (GB), Columbo (USA), Mike Stone (USA), Derrick (D), Bullitt (USA), Philip Marlowe (USA), Matula (D), Hercule Poirot (Belgian – British author (Agatha Christie)), Miss Marple (GB)

Reasons for the popularity of police and detective series and films:
- suspense
- more exciting than real life for most people
- plenty of action as a rule
- some detectives are interesting characters
- background often interesting (Victorian London for Sherlock Holmes, San Francisco for Mike Stone etc.)

While-reading tasks

How does this dialogue differ from the kind of dialogue you normally practise in school? ◀ p. 36

e.g. more short forms and incomplete sentences, questions are not answered, several topics mixed together, some non-standard grammar.

Why might Jill not welcome a visit from the police? Think of as many reasons as you can, and when you have seen or read the whole episode, check whether you guessed right. ◀ p. 37

e.g.
- most people are upset when the police knock at their front door
- doesn't like the police
- may be involved in criminal activities
- may have something (drugs?) hidden in her flat
- may be hiding someone the police are looking for

How would you react if you were given this kind of present? Is Jill being fair when she calls it "junk"? ◀ p. 38

Possible reactions:
- pretty, nice souvenir, typical of Spain
- will just lie around, cheap, probably not even made in Spain.

The doll probably is junk, but if Jill still loved Leo she wouldn't call it junk.

Why this question? *(i.e. D'you drink Scotch?)* ◀ p. 38

The policeman is reminding his partners that they will be given a bottle of whisky by Sgt. Boyden if they catch Leo before the CID find him – and they have found Leo.

Explain Sgt. Boyden's little joke here. Is he behaving professionally? If not, why not? ◀ p. 39

Of course Tommy Wood can't be arrested for breathing, but Sgt Boyden is angry because Leo has got away, and because of the fuss Tommy Wood is making. The sergeant is only human, after all, and he allows his feelings to get the better of him, which is unprofessional. He probably doesn't have any real reason to arrest Wood at this point, although he had been talking to a wanted man, so he can't actually name the charge against Wood, and makes a joke instead.

Sgt. Boyden *says* the barkeeper has done the right thing, but his tone of voice seems to tell a different story. What might the sergeant be thinking? ◀ p. 40

The sergeant is probably thinking that the barkeeper should at least have tried to stop Grey attacking Jill. He seems to have been entirely passive throughout. However, it is questionable whether it is a good idea for private citizens to "have a go" in such circumstances.

p. 41

What is Sgt. Boyden's little joke here?

Sgt. Boyden knows that Grey owns a sports shop, so there could be a pair of trainers in the box, but Grey wouldn't be so worried if this was the case.

p. 42

Explain the irony here.

Leo feels that he has been partly responsible for Tony Grey's arrest, and he probably thinks Chris Darrow deserved to be attacked. He thinks he has earned his "welcome back" from Sgt. Boyden, who then arrests him for something which Leo doesn't consider a crime. Grey's crimes, particularly his drug dealing, are something which Leo *does* consider serious.

p. 42

Why does the policeman grin?

Because he knows that Sgt. Beech is about to lose his bet/be embarrassed/have to admit failure/admit that the uniformed police have been more successful.

p. 42

Does Sgt. Beech mean what he says?

No. He means the exact opposite. He is going to hate it/feel humiliated/lose quite a large sum of money.

p. 42

Why does Sgt. Boyden say this?

Sgt. Boyden feels bitter because the CID are generally supposed to be cleverer/more efficient than the uniformed police, who are thought (by the CID and possibly by the public) to be a bit slow ("plodding") and not very imaginative. So "CID standards" would normally be higher – but not this time.

p. 42

Why mention Jill?

This is Sergeant Beech's last chance to salvage a bit of dignity. If Sgt. Boyden hadn't found Jill as well as the other suspects, it would mean they hadn't cleared up the case.

Activities — Characters p. 42

1. Collect quotations from the text which throw light on the characters of the two sergeants. Why do you think there is rivalry between them? Whose side are you on, and why? What role do their different jobs play?

Sample quotations:

Sgt. Beech	Sgt. Boyden
Remember me? (thinks of himself as important) . I'm gonna love this (will not find it all easy to "eat humble pie" and admit that he has lost the bet)	Brilliant! (sense of irony, hard to control his feelings) Right. You're nicked (arrests Wood for prodding him in the chest rather than any real offence – not very professional

Eh, you remember that breach of bail ... (very unwilling to admit he has been beaten, prepared to try almost anything to avoid paying up)	in this case – however, Sgt. Boyden generally does everything by the book in this instalment – a good policemean) Nothing by CID standards, 'course. (has something of an inferiority complex as far as the CID is concerned)

2. Make notes on Jill, then compare notes with your neighbour. Discuss points of agreement and disagreement.

Points which could be made:
- Fairly good-looking, sexy
- rather shallow emotionally – finds it easy to reject her well-meaning husband in favour of another man
- naive – thinks she can meddle in drugs without getting hurt, and then talk her way out of trouble
- no signs of a sense of humour
- possibly not very intelligent

3. List all the verbal and visual information you can about Leo, and write a short character sketch. Then select relevant information for the report on him in the police computer, and write it out in note form.

Leo is a big, strong man, accustomed to manual work (building work in Spain). He loves his wife, and considers himself an honest person. He is dead against drugs. He is good-natured and sentimental even "sweet" as a rule, particularly as far as Jill is concerned, but he becomes violent when he thinks an injustice has been done. He is short-tempered and not very bright. He would be likely to try and settle an argument with his fists.

Notes for the computer:
Leo Morrison
– not a serious criminal
– unlikely to be involved in drugs offences
– record of assault/ABH (actual bodily harm)
– check out in connection with fights in pubs etc.

1. Can you say anything about the level of formal education of the various characters?

◀ **The spoken language p. 43**

Sgt. Beech: Probably university education.
Sgt. Boyden: good secondary school education.
Jill: Similar education to Sgt. Boyden probably
Tony Grey: Well-educated.
Leo: Poorly educated. Almost certainly did badly in school, left without any qualifications.

2. What differences are there between the kind of English you are learning to speak and the English in the film?

School English
correct grammar
complete sentences
set dialogues
limited number of short forms
neutral accent

The Bill
Some characters use incorrect grammar
dialogues interrupted
mainly London accents
extensive use of short forms

3. Most of the speakers use versions of London or Estuary English. What are some of the main features of this variety? Leo has a classic London accent.

Some features of cockney English:
- missing initial /h/
- contrast between e.g. thin and /fin/ is missing
- paws = [pɔəz]
- milk = [mɪʊk]
- paper = [paɪpa]
- g missing in -ing

> **You are the script-writers p. 43**

1. Imagine that Leo, Tony Grey and Jill are let out on bail, along with Chris Darrow when he comes out of hospital. What kind of meetings might take place? Would the police have to be called? Or an ambulance? Write the script for a scene, act it and record it on video if possible.

Likely attitudes at the start of the scene:
Leo: sure he is in the right, wants everything cleared up properly. Will become violent if things don't go his way.
Tony Grey: Will probably want nothing more to do with Jill or Chris. Likely to become nasty/threatening if they try to blame him for their problems.
Jill: sees that she has been naive, and that Leo is a much better partner than Chris.
Chris: May want revenge on Leo. May or may not see the error of his ways.

2. A local government official is suspected of corruption. Then he is arrested on a drunken driving charge. He complains to Sgt. Beech (with whom he plays golf) that he is being victimised by the uniformed police (Sgt. Boyden and his team). Choose an aspect of this scenario which interests you. Write the script, act it and record it on video if possible.

Example:
On the golf course. Official explains that he has the feeling that he is being victimised. Sgt. Beech says the uniformed police are just doing their job. Official says everybody was drunk on the night in question – only he was stopped.
The corruptions charges are also ridiculous. Sgt. Beech turns less friendly – says they have evidence of bribery in connection with a contract for a new school or hospital in the town.

Satirical comedy: *Yes, Prime Minister: The Smoke Screen*

About the text

The view of the way in which the British government works is incredibly cynical. The Prime Minister will do anything to get his tax cut, even using an idealistic Health Minister as a pawn in his game, and ultimately corrupting him. Health and moral issues mean little when set against the wealth and influence of the tobacco industry.

Synopsis of the text

The Minister of Health, Peter Thorn, comes in to ask whether the Prime Minister is prepared to support him in a drastic campaign to reduce spoking. At first the Prime Minister seems to be luke-warm. The Health Minister reminds him of the health risks, but the Prime Minister says that the Treasury would resist the campaign because it needs the money brought in by the tax on tobacco. He then changes course and says that he would like the Health Minister to make speeches about his plans. He explains to his Private Secretary that there is no chance of the anti-smoking campaign succeeding. He merely wants to put the Treasury under pressure so that they will agree to a tax cut which will make him more popular.
Sir Humphrey, his senior civil servant, laughs at the idea that smoking could be eliminated. He claims that no causative link between smoking and killer diseases has ever been proved. He points out that smokers not only contribute a great deal of money to the economy through taxes, they also save the country a great deal of money by dying young. The jobs of thousands of people depend upon tobacco in in one way or another. In addition, the tobacco companies are also great sponsors of sport.
The Minister for Sport comes in, having heard rumours of a possible attack on the tobacco industry, for which he acts as a paid consultant. He is a heavy smoker himself.
At an informal meeting in their club, senior civil servants agree that doctors are bound to be biased on the matter, and cannot be trusted to act wisely. As far as they are concerned, tobacco revenues are much more important than the health issue.
Dr. Thorn comes back to the Prime Minister's office, excited about the support he is receiving from leaders of the medical profession. He finds that the Prime Minister is now much less enthusiastic, and says that he will have to resign if his scheme comes to nothing.
Sir Humphrey drops in to confirm that the tax cuts the Prime Minister wants have now become possible. This is the result of Treasury fears about loss of tobacco revenue. They see the Prime Minister's tax cut as the lesser of two evils. It is quite clear that the Prime Minister will only get his tax cut if the anti-smoking campaign is dropped.
The Prime Minister is very worried about the Health Minister's threatened resignation, but Sir Humphrey reminds him that there is a senior post vacant in the Treasury at the moment, for which Dr. Thorn would be the ideal candidate. As this is a big promotion for him, he accepts.

This leaves a vacancy at the Ministry of Health, which is offered to the Minister for Sport, in spite of his own poor health as a heavy smoker, and the fact that he is a consultant for the tobacco industry. He accepts, on condition that he will not have to attack the tobacco industry.

Unterrichts-empfehlungen

Einsatzmöglichkeiten:
Der Text und die Filmfassung lassen sich in unterschiedlichen Kontexten einsetzen. Abgesehen von unserer Reihe zu *Media and Television* eignet sich *The Smoke Screen* vor allem als Teil einer Reihe zu den Themenkomplexen *British Government* bzw. *Democracy in the UK* nicht nur als Ausdruck einer satirisch geprägten Sicht, sondern auch als – nach Meinung vieler Kritiker – durchaus mit realistischen Elementen gekennzeichnete Darstellung der politischen Szene, in der demokratische und moralische Ideale und Ansprüche nur zu schnell lobbyistischen Interessen und kurzfristigen politischen Zielen geopfert werden oder von Seiten der Ministerialbürokratie mit dem Ziel, Besitzstände zu wahren, abgeblockt werden.

Unterrichtsverfahren:
1. Der Einstieg erfolgt über die unten beschriebene *pre-reading task*, die unmittelbar auf den thematischen Schwerpunkt des Textes hinarbeitet. Auf die Lektüre des transkribierten Auszugs kann nun, nachdem der Kurs sich bereits mit mehreren Videoauszügen aktiv beschäftigt hat, verzichtet werden. Jedoch sollte vor der Auseinandersetzung mit dem Videoauszug zunächst der einleitende Text besprochen und, wo dies notwendig erscheint, verdeutlicht werden. Ohne Kenntnis der Rivalität zwischen der Ministerialbürokratie (vertreten durch Sir Humphrey) und den Politikern (vertreten durch Jim Hacker) ist die Serie *Yes, Prime Minister* nicht verständlich.
2. Nach ein- oder zweimaligem Vorspielen des Auszugs wird mit dem Kurs eine inhaltliche Zusammenfassung vorgenommen. Dabei ist der transkribierte Text für sprachliche und inhaltliche Erläuterungen hilfreich. Die eventuell erforderliche Pause für das Vorspulen zum zweiten Teil kann für die intensive Lektüre des Zwischentextes (S. 47) und damit zur Sicherung der Kenntnis des weiteren Handlungsverlaufs genutzt werden.
3. Im Anschluss daran lassen sich die *while-reading tasks* angehen. Hierbei werden die einzelnen Kurzszenen näher untersucht. Daraus ergibt sich die Notwendigkeit, bei bestimmten Szenen das Band zu stoppen, Teile mehrfach zu zeigen, um im Sinne des Ziels der *media literacy* den Kursmitgliedern Gelegenheit zu detaillierter Betrachtung zu geben.
4. Die sich daran anschließende Erarbeitung der Aufgaben zu *The Implications* (S. 49) lässt sich vorteilhaft in Partnerarbeit im Unterricht vornehmen. Es ist sinnvoll, sich zunächst auf die Aufgaben 1 und 2 zu konzentrieren, da die dritte Aufgabenstellung aufgrund ihres kommentierenden Charakters zeitlich aufwendiger ist und u.U. eine Verlegung in die häusliche Vorbereitung für die folgende Stunde erforderlich macht.
5. Die Auseinandersetzung mit der Sequenz sollte nicht ohne Vorspielen der kompletten Folge abschließen. Dies kann durchaus

die Motivation sowie die inhaltlichen Voraussetzungen für den Kurs schaffen, sich im Zusammenhang eines anderen Themas mit einer anderen Folge auseinander zu setzen (sich dazu anbietende Themen der Fernsehserie sind u.a.: Das britische Erziehungswesen; Abrüstung; Europa; Internationale Beziehungen; Wahlkampf).
6. Zum Abschluss der Besprechung dieses Videoauszugs kann eine Diskussion mit verteilten Rollen zum Thema *Should smoking be banned?* stattfinden.

Assignments

Pre-reading task

Everyone knows that smoking is bad for health – even if every smoker has heard of someone who smoked forty cigarettes a day and lived to be ninety! Why do you think smoking is still so popular, and why do you think governments are so unwilling to take really *serious* steps to reduce tobacco consumption?

◀ Before you watch or read ... p. 44

Reasons for popularity
- cinema and other advertising
- positive images linked with major brands
- counts as an "adult" thing to do
- a kind of protest against parents
- addictive

Reasons for lack of action:
- Tobacco revenue
- Jobs
- Influence of the tobacco industry
- Sports and other kinds of sponsorship

While-reading tasks

Why do you think the Prime Minister asks for this summary?

◀ p. 44

Because he hasn't read the Health Minister's paper.

These three expressions all mean much the same: Why does the Prime Minister more or less repeat himself here?

◀ p. 44

He wants to indicate that action is not likely to take place until the distant future, if then. Incidentally, this is the kind of language Sir Humphrey uses when he is employing delaying tactics.

Why the pause before *again*?

◀ p. 45

The Prime Minister is on the point of admitting that he hasn't read the Health Minister's paper yet. The *again* saves the day.

Is this the real reason for the Prime Minister's unwillingness to support the Minister of Health publicly?

◀ p. 45

No. He knows that the Health Minister's campaign is bound to fail. It would be bad for his reputation if he was associated with a failed campaign.

p. 45	**Why does the Prime Minister correct himself?**
	A cigarette paper is the piece of paper which holds a (hand-rolled) cigarette together.
p. 45	**Why is the Prime Minister so keen on tax cuts?**
	Because he believes that tax cuts will make him and his government more popular.
p. 45	**Why does Sir Humphrey laugh two or three times during this scene?**
	Because he can't believe the Prime Minister is serious. He regards the proposals as silly, even insane.
p. 46	**Why does Sir Humphrey agree with the Prime Minister here?**
	He is agreeing with the idea of *contemplating* the proposal, not actually supporting or implementing it. (He often appears to agree (line of least resistance) at the start of a discussion, but later twists the argument to suit his own position.)
p. 46	**Whose argument is this? (i.e. no causative link between smoking and disease)**
	The tobacco industry's.
p. 46	**Do you agree? Give examples where different sets of statistics prove different things.**
	Suggestions in connection with motoring: Car manufacturers claim that ABS makes cars safer. In fact cars with ABS are involved in more accidents than cars without. Not everyone believes that stricter alcohol limits will significantly reduce the number of accidents – it may only lead to the closing of country pubs. Building more roads does not necessarily reduce traffic jams – it also increases the amount of traffic on the roads.
p. 47	**What does the Prime Minister's tone of voice tell you here?**
	It indicates that he does not think the news of support for Dr. Thorn's plans is marvellous at all. On the contrary. It looks as if Dr. Thorn might actually succeed.
p. 47	**What do we know about the Treasury?**
	That they will never willingly give up a penny of their revenues, from whatever source.
p. 48	**What is *ironic* in this scene?**
	Mr Potts is totally unsuitable for the job of Health Minister. He is a heavy smoker who works as a consultant for the tobacco industry. He is being offered the job because it is certain that he will not attack the tobacco industry, although smoking is such a major health risk.

Why does Mr Potts say this?

As a consultant for the tobacco industry he is committed to supporting it, not attacking it. If he was forced to attack the tobacco industry, he would have to give up a nice source of extra income.

◀ p. 48

Activities

1. The Prime Minister says he will "definitely lose" the battle against the tobacco lobby, and he doesn't even seem to mind very much. Why not?

◀ Watching (or reading) for gist p. 49

His plan is to allow Dr Thorn to frighten the Treasury into thinking that they are likely to lose most of their tobacco income, so that they will be quite happy, when this turns out not to be the case, to grant him his cherished tax increase.

2. Summarise Sir Humphrey's arguments in favour of letting smokers go on killing themselves at the present rate.

– Smokers who die young save the country money on pensions and medical treatment in old age.
– Cigarette taxes pay for a third of the cost of the National Health Service.
– Smokers help to save the lives of others, while possibly endangering their own health.
– They should be considered as public benefactors.

3. Why is the Prime Minister so worried about Dr Thorn's resignation threat, and what solution is suggested by Sir Humphrey?

The Prime Minister fears that if Dr. Thorn resigns, people will find out that he did so because the Prime Minister would not support his crusade against the tobacco industry. This would make him unpopular. Sir Humphrey's solution is to "kick Dr. Thorn upstairs", i.e. to promote him to a position where he will not be able to do any damage.

1. Everything Dr Thorn says about the effects of tobacco is true. It is also true that the tobacco industry employs a lot of people, generates a lot of revenue for the the governmnent and sponsors sports and the arts. If you were a politician, what would your position be on this issue?

◀ The implications p. 49

2. Should Dr Thorn have accepted his promotion?

For accepting:
The Treasury is powerful – he may be better able to influence the affairs of the nation from his new position
Better pay
More prestige

Against accepting:
Knows the promotion is for the wrong reasons
Would no longer be directly concerned with health
Should resist temptation and stand up for his principles

Writing a script ▶ p. 49

Imagine that the PM's student daughter is involved in a protest against a new runway at an English airport. She and other protestors intend to take off their clothes and stand in front of the bulldozers. How will the PM and Sir Humphrey react? Will they be able to stop her? What are the arguments for and against the new runway? Write and practise your own script.

Arguments for new runway:
- jobs, communications, boost for local businesses, good for the image of the town

Against:
- noise/exhaust pollution, destruction of countryside, properties near airport will lose value

Additional assignment

Collect articles from the British, American and/or German press about possible legislation concerning tobacco, alcohol or other drugs. Write a statement explaining the issues in the area you have selected, and add your own views.

Costume drama: *Pride and Prejudice*   based on the novel by Jane Austen

About the text

It is not possible for readers and/or viewers to gain an impression of the novel as a whole from this short extract. The main love story, between Mr Darcy and Elizabeth is only hinted at. However, the scenes with the unfortunate Mr Collins, who proposes to another local girl and is accepted only days after Elizabeth turns him down, have a more or less self-contained story line of their own. They illustrate Jane Austen's talent for both affectionate and satirical character portrayal, and her matchless ear for dialogue.

Author

Jane Austen (1775-1817) was the daughter of a clergyman, George Austen, who taught her at home and encouraged her to read widely. She was the sixth child in a family of seven.
Her life was on the whole uneventful, apart from occasional trips to Bath or London. She never married, but was surrounded by a large, lively and affectionate family, including her beloved sister Cassandra and a number of nieces and nephews.
Although her letters are quite frank, she deliberately avoided anything at all intimate in her novels. The range of her work is limited. Two famous quotations from her letters will help readers to understand what she was trying to do:
"3 or 4 families in a Country Village is the very thing to work on."
"The little bit (two inches wide) of Ivory on which I work with so fine a brush, as produces little effect after much labour."
On the whole readers and critics have not agreed that Jane Austen worked to "little effect." In fact, her six main novels are consi-

dered by many to be among the best works of fiction in English. Her ability to create attractive (and unattractive) three-dimensional characters, and to carry the plot along via a series of conversations, are unsurpassed. While apparently describing the surface of life, she deals in fact with life itself. She can be both sympathetic and satirical as the occasion demands.
Main works: *Sense and Sensibility* (1811), *Pride and Prejudice* (1813), *Mansfield Park* (1814), *Emma* (1816). *Northanger Abbey* and *Persuasion* were published posthumously in 1818.
In the 1990's a number of good films and television series based on Jane Austen's novels led to renewed interest in the author and her works.

Synopsis of the text

At the start of the scene Mr Bennet reads out a letter from Mr Collins, a relative of his, who intends to pay the Bennets a visit. Mr Collins will one day inherit the Bennets' home, and feels that it is his duty to make amends by getting to know the Bennets.
Mr Collins is a pedantic clergyman, obsessed by his imagined link with the aristocracy through Lady Catherine de Bourgh, who has obtained a living for him at Huntsford Rectory. The Bennets make fun of his snobbery and wordy style of speaking and writing. He is not at all the sort of young man any of the daughters would want to marry. He is not smart enough for the younger daughters, who prefer officers in the militia, or cultured enough for the older daughters, Jane and Elizabeth, both of whom will eventually marry wealthy young gentlemen of good family. Mr Collins soon makes it clear that he is planning to marry one of the Bennet girls. Mrs Bennet explains to him that Jane is already spoken for, so he decides to marry Elizabeth, the second daughter and heroine of the novel. During his long proposal speech, which Elizabeth tries in vain to interrupt, he mentions "the violence of (his) affections" only after listing every other possible unromantic reason for marrying. When Elizabeth turns him down, Mrs Bennet is absolutely furious, and insists that her husband makes Elizabeth accept him.
However, Mr Bennet, who loves Elizabeth and knows very well that she could never be happy with Mr Collins, says: "Your mother will never see you again if you do not marry Mr Collins, and I will never see you again if you do."

Unterrichts-empfehlungen

Der Auszug aus dem Filmskript ist recht anspruchsvoll. Als Verfilmung eines literarischen Werkes führt dieser Text im Vergleich zu den anderen Videoauszügen dieser Sammlung in eine ganz andere Welt und verlangt von der Lerngruppe ein Sich-Einfühlen in einen zeitlich und kulturell völlig anderen Kontext. Dies ist keineswegs leicht, vor allem wenn das Videoband nicht zur Verfügung steht. Die drei *pre-viewing tasks* (S. 50) versuchen eine Brücke zur Welt des späten 18. und frühen 19. Jahrhunderts zu spannen um den Kursmitgliedern ein differenziertes Bild jenseits des einfachen Klischees, dass in diesem Auszug die Personen und ihre Handlungen „anders" sind, zu ermöglichen. Der Einbezug eventueller Vorkenntnisse aus der Lektüre ähnlicher literarischer Texte, z.B. im Deutsch- oder Literaturunterricht, kann hilfreich sein. Ebenso sind Rückbezüge zum Geschichts- bzw. Sozialkundeunterricht möglich. U.U. sind dort die Lebensbedingungen jener Zeit, vor allem auch in Bezug auf die Rolle der Frau, unter unterschiedlichen Fragestellungen thematisiert worden.

Im Rahmen einer Sammelphase werden Erwartungen und Vorkenntnisse formuliert, die zur Auseinandersetzung mit dem Videoauszug hinführen. Ein einmaliges Vorspielen des Bandes ohne Blick auf die Textvorlage im Schülerbuch erscheint sinnvoll um anschließend mit dem Kurs eine grobe Rekonstruktion des Inhalts zu versuchen. Mit dieser Form der Texterschließung kann man herausfinden, inwieweit der Kurs bereits in der Lage ist, schon beim ersten Betrachten wesentliche Teile des Inhalts sinnvoll zu rekonstruieren.

Im Rahmen eines zweiten Vorspielens werden die *while-viewing tasks* gezielt untersucht, wobei ein Stoppen des Bandes an einzelnen Stellen mit entsprechendem Wiedervorspielen bestimmter Passagen erforderlich sein wird. Im Anschluss können in Form von Gruppenarbeit mit arbeitsteiligen Aufgabenaufträgen die vier Fragen auf S. 55 zu *Characters and relationships* erarbeitet, vorgetragen und diskutiert werden. Die beiden produktionsorientierten Aufgaben *Advice for Mr Collins* sowie *Elizabeth and Jane* lassen sich aufgrund der zur Lösung erforderlichen Zeit vorteilhaft in die Hausaufgabe verlegen und in der folgenden Stunde ausführlich besprechen. Statt nur die eine oder andere Lösung im Kurs zu besprechen, ließe sich als alternativer Weg ein Gruppenarbeitsverfahren denken, in dem in jeder Gruppe die Kursmitglieder sich gegenseitig ihre Textproduktion zu einem der beiden Themen vorlesen und kommentieren und die ihnen am gelungensten erscheinende Lösung dem gesamten Kurs vorstellen und dabei auch ihre Auswahl sinnvoll begründen. Dies Verfahren nimmt allerdings Unterrichtszeit in Anspruch, ist jedoch in Bezug auf Lernziele wie selbstständiges Lernen, Selbstkorrektur und Begründungen finden, formulieren und vortragen, ergiebig. Die abschließende Aufgabe *Words v. pictures* gibt dem Kurs Gelegenheit zu einer abschließenden Auswertung und zur Kommentierung der möglichen Umsetzungen von Worten in Bilder. Dabei kann natürlich auch in einem zweiten Schritt über die Textvorlage hinausgegangen und die generelle Problematik der Umsetzung literarischer Vorlagen in einen Film diskutiert und andere Texte/Verfilmungen hinzugezogen werden.

Assignments

Pre-reading tasks

Before you watch or read ... p. 50

1. What kind of story do you expect when you look at the young couple in the photograph?

Some of the options:
- boy meets girl
- romantic fiction
- historical love story
- tall, dark and handsome stranger arrives on the scene
- old-fashioned, not likely to appeal to modern readers/viewers

2. What was life like for women in those days? How has it changed?

Points that could be made:
- virtually no legal status
- hardly any jobs a "lady" could do (except become a governess – often an unpleasant job with doubtful status)
- absolutely essential to get married, if possible to a gentleman with plenty of money.
- large families – no birth control
- servants to do the hard work in wealthier families
- otherwise drudgery

3. Were the "good old days" really better – or worse? List some good and bad aspects of life early in the 19th century, and talk about them. Would the Bennets have had a bathroom, for example?

Some points covered above. Also worth mentioning:
- almost certainly no bathroom in a home like the Bennets' – hygiene well below modern standards generally
- medicine in its infancy
- travel very difficult – most people did not venture very far from home
- country life for well-off people nevertheless very pleasant. England is dotted with the large houses with extensive grounds in which they lived
- gap between rich and poor, gentry and non-gentry very large

While-reading tasks

Why does Mr Bennet say this? (i.e. *There, Mrs Bennet*) ◀ p. 51

Mrs Bennet assumes Mr Collins must be an odious man (because he will inherit their house one day) although she has never met him. The fact that he wants to "heal the breach" between himself and the Bennets should enable her to think more kindly of him. She does not at this point realise that he is coming to look for a wife.

What do you think of Mr Collins' style? ◀ p. 51

- Uses a lot of long words
- misses no opportunity to put in an adjective
- long, involved sentences
- style similar to a sermon in church
- self-centred
- snobbish

Who do you think Dawkins is? ◀ p. 51

The coachman.

Mr Bennet has come to the conclusion, based on the letter, that he will be able to make fun of Mr Collins. What could his reasons be? ◀ p. 52

Any of the points listed in connection with Mr Collins' style, plus the fact that he doesn't seem to be at all aware of the effect that this style may have on other people

p. 52 ▸ Why does Mr Collins say this? (i.e. *Perhaps especially the eldest Miss Bennet*)

He already has his eye on Jane as a potential Mrs Collins. (She is felt to be the most conventionally beautiful of the Bennet girls, but is not so lively and intelligent as Elizabeth). He is tentatively asking if Jane is "available". Mrs Bennet knows exactly what he means.

p. 52 ▸ Do you think Mr Collins really likes walking?

Definitely not. He just wants a chance to talk to (in modern terms 'chat up') Elizabeth.

p. 53 ▸ Why is Elizabeth so nervous?

She knows only too well what Mr Collins wants to say to her, and would like to be able to avoid an embarrassing scene.

p. 53 ▸ Why is Mrs Bennet so insistent?

She knows that Mr Collins intends to propose, and sees this as a wonderful chance to get one of her daughters "off her hands." Elizabeth's feelings do not matter to her – she is incapable of appreciating how unhappy Elizabeth would be with Mr Collins (and he with her!).

p. 53 ▸ Which word shows us that Mr Collins is honest?

Almost – he had his eye on Jane until he found out that she was spoken for.

p. 53 ▸ Is he being honest here?

Not entirely. He has taken the trouble to find out about Elizabeth's financial situation (it would be the same for the other daughters) before coming to visit the Bennets. If he was "perfectly indifferent" he would not have bothered to do so.

p. 54 ▸ Why doesn't Mr Collins accept Elizabeth's refusal?

He has read that it is usual in such cases for the lady to refuse at first, fully intending to accept later.

p. 54 ▸ What is missing from this list?

There is no mention of Elizabeth's feelings. Instead we have a list of Mr Collins' 'qualifications' as a husband, and a cruel (but fairly realistic) assessment of Elizabeth's chances in the marriage market, as a girl who will inherit very little money and no property.

Activities

Characters and relationships p. 55 ▸
1. How do you think Mr Bennet feels about
   a) his wife and
   b) his second daughter Elizabeth?
   Back up your answer with reference to the text or to visual clues.

a) Mr Bennet cannot take his wife seriously. He addresses her almost as if she is a child who may react unpredictably. No visual marks of affection between them.

b) Mr Bennet loves Elizabeth. Senses her intelligence. Note the little chat about Mr Collins's character as he arrives, and his defence of her when Mrs Bennet is trying to insist that Elizabeth marries Mr Collins.

2. Jane Austen (and the makers of the television version) clearly intend us to disapprove of Mr Collins. What exactly is wrong with his character? Why does Mr Bennet support Elizabeth's decision to refuse him?

Points which could be made:
- Any of the points already covered in connection with his style.
- Assumes he must be attractive as a husband because of his connections to the aristocracy and relative prosperity.
- Never asks himself whether his personal qualities are likely to appeal to a young woman like Elizabeth
- Blind to attempts to make fun of him.
- Not physically attractive, clumsy.
- Not a 'gentleman' in the full sense of the word. Depends on Lady Catherine for his status.

3. Elizabeth Bennet is generally agreed to be a most attractive character in every way. Why do you think this is?

This is not an easy question to answer. There is no doubt that the author identifies with Elizabeth and sympathises with her. She is intelligent, lively, has a sense of humour and a lot of initiative, and would only consider marrying a man she can truly love, in spite of the fact that "Mr Right" may never come along. She is not without human weaknesses – for example she falls for the villain Wickham, and believes his dishonest version of the events which led to his break with Darcy, the wealthy and generally very attractive young man Elizabeth will eventually marry. Jane Austen's charting of their feelings towards one another is masterly. They develop gradually from pride, even insults on Darcy's part and consequent dislike and misunderstanding on Elizabeth's, to eventual reconciliation and true love.

4. There has been no mention of Mary, the third or middle daughter, although she appears in the video extract. Have you any idea what she might be like?

(only possible for students who have seen the video)
Mary is a bookish girl, who has various 'accomplishments' such as playing the piano, but she has little sense of appropriateness (what to play, when to stop), and is entirely humourless, a serious fault in Jane Austen's book.

Imagine that you were able to listen to Mr Collins' proposal as "a fly on the wall." Write a letter to him telling him what you think he did wrong, and how he might make a better job of it next time.

◀ Advice for Mr Collins p. 55

Most of the points which could be made appear in the answer to the question: *What is missing from this list*, and in the notes about Mr Collins' character.

Elizabeth and Jane p. 55

Elizabeth and Jane are very fond of one another. Write a scene in which they talk about Mr Collins' proposal before going to bed that evening.

It will help students to write a good scene if they are told that Jane is generally prepared to believe the best of people – even Mr Collins, but she will surely be on her sister's side over the refusal to marry him.

Words v. pictures p. 55

In what ways do the pictures bring the words to life and add layers of meaning? Were there any examples of camera technique which you thought were particularly clever and/or successful? Please describe and comment on anything of this kind which struck you.

Likely scenes:
- the transfer from Mr Bennet reading Mr Collins' letter to his actual arrival near the beginning. Clever shift from the fairly 'remote' letter, to the coach journey, to the arrival of Mr Collins in person. The scene deals with both time and distance very neatly.
- The game of quoits, with the camera following Mr Collins' gaze as he sizes up the Bennet girls as potential wives. An element of humour here – we know what he is thinking.

Postscript: The Media – Watchdog or Rottweiler?

About the text

This text was written by the editor in order to counterbalance to some extent the generally positive choice of material and attitudes to newspapers and television which emerge from the rest of the book. It was only natural to choose high quality material on the whole for the examples.

The students who ask questions in this scene raise most of the main criticisms of the media which are voiced today. Some teachers working with the book will agree with almost everything they say, others will feel that the students are unnecessarily aggressive and negative. The truth, as far as the editor is concerned, lies somewhere between the two extremes.

Synopsis of the text

The editor of a tabloid newspaper visits a school near her home. She is subjected to hostile questioning by senior pupils. They ask her first why it was in the public interest to publish a picture of an MP kissing a woman who was not his wife. The reply is that someone whose party believes in family values should observe them himself – and it is in the public interest to know if he doesn't. A question about the use of a telephoto lens to obtain the photograph is answered indirectly. The newspaper needs to sell three million copies a day, and compromising photos are more interesting for the reader.

The next question refers to the fact that newspaper owners may influence editorial content. The editor says she has complete freedom to print what she wants, but has to admit that nothing which would clash with the owner's views has in fact appeared in her newspaper.

Another student asks about reality TV programmes which are produced by the same company which produces her newspapers. The editor says that anyone who doesn't like the programmes can turn off their television. She admits that she watches very little television anyway, and is criticised for writing off people with less demanding jobs than hers as couch potatoes.

The editor counters by listing worthwhile achievements of her newspaper and associated television company, such as consumer affairs programmes on TV and campaigns of various kinds in connection with dangerous drugs, faulty cars etc. They also raise money for charitable purposes.

Another student asks about cigarette advertising in the newspaper and its colour supplement. She is told that there would be no colour supplement without the income from advertisements, and no formula I car races either.

The editor then establishes that many of the students actually read the teenage magazine which comes with the Saturday edition of her newspaper, and they all watch television. She sees it as the teacher's job to warn students about the dangers of the media, and her job to produce an interesting and successful newspaper.

Unterrichts-empfehlungen

Der abschließende Text des Schülerbuchs sollte mit verteilten Rollen vorgelesen werden. Um eine gewisse Vertrautheit mit dem Text herzustellen, ist etwas Zeit für die Vorbereitung des Lesens sinnvoll. Die anderen Kursmitglieder lesen ebenfalls den Text, wobei sie bereits mit Blick auf die Aufgabe *The media in the firing line* an die Arbeit gehen und beim Lesen bzw. Verfolgen des Vorlesens durch Markieren relevanter Stellen die anschließende inhaltliche Erarbeitung vorbereiten. Im Anschluss werden in Partnerarbeit die erkundeten Passagen verglichen und auf eine Folie übertragen. Dabei werden zunächst nur die beiden Spalten für *criticisms* und *Ms Fairbanks answer* ausgefüllt, bevor die Spalte *comment* stichwortartig gefüllt wird. Einige Gruppen präsentieren ihre Ergebnisse, die im Kursverband kritisch diskutiert werden. Aufgabe 2 (Seite 59) lässt sich im Unterricht in Form von Rede und Gegenrede erarbeiten. Die verbleibenden Aufgaben zu *Ethics* werden im Paket von einer Kurshälfte in Form einer schriftlichen Hausaufgabe gelöst. Dies erscheint deswegen sinnvoll, weil Teil 1 eine komplexe Aufgabenstellung aufweist. Die andere Hälfte des Kurses befasst sich im Rahmen ihrer Hausaufgabe mit der Aufgabe zu *Pressures*. Hier ist für eine angemessene Lösung die Hinzunahme weiterer Materials erforderlich. Ob die abschließende Stunde nach Präsentation der Hausaufgaben eine Auswertung etwa unter dem Aspekt *What were your most important/helpful/disturbing findings?* vornimmt, entscheidet der zur Verfügung stehende Zeitrahmen. Sollte die Kursleitung sich zu einer solchen Auswertungsstunde entschließen, erscheint es sinnvoll, dabei nicht nur inhaltliche, sondern auch methodische Aspekte mit einzubeziehen. Vor allem kann dabei auf eine Einschätzung des Lerngewinns in Bezug auf den Umgang mit visuellen Texten eingegangen werden.

Assignments

While-reading tasks

p. 57 ▶ Can you think of a similar saying in German?

Wes' Brot ich ess'.
Des' Lied ich sing'.

p. 57 ▶ Is this answer satisfactory? Give reasons.

It is a clever answer. Of course everyone can turn off the television, but many people do not, and some people become addicted to chat and game shows etc. If everyone responsible for TV programmes thought like this, there would be no quality television at all.

How would our newspapers and magazines look without advertising? ◀ p. 58

Much thinner and/or more expensive to buy, much less varied and colourful in layout. Less entertainment value, more independent reporting possibly.

Activities

1. List the main criticisms of the media which occur in the course of the text. How does Ms Fairbanks answer each of these criticisms, if at all? Comment on her replies. Set your work out in three columns.

◀ The media in the firing line p. 58

Criticisms	Answer	Comments
intrusion into privacy	in the public interest	
use of telephoto lenses	necessary for interesting pictures	
owner dictates policy	editorial freedom	
rubbishy TV	viewers can turn off their sets	
TV is for couch potatoes	good consumer programmes, investigative journalism, money raised for charity	
too much advertising	necessary in order to finance newspapers and magazines	
tobacco advertising bad	tobacco sponsorship of sport	
TV panders to our lowest instincts	teacher's job to warn of media sins	

1. Where does "in the public interest" become "intrusion into privacy"? Describe and comment on some real or imagined borderline cases.

◀ Ethics p. 59

The death of Princess Diana would be a good starting point.
Inevitable public interest in photos of the crash scene etc., but there were no really important political or other consequences (except the usual threats to limit the freedom of the press).
Any scandal involving a politician raises the question whether a bad husband (for example) can be a good politician, and whether we have the right to know about his (private) sins or not.

2. How far do you agree with the editor's final statement?

Mainly a personal answer, but students should be reminded that most of the "rubbish" we see and read is the result of the freedom of the press. If the "rubbish" were repressed, other more valuable things might be repressed, too. The same arguments apply in cases of privacy. The right to privacy would certainly mean the right to get away with murder (literally or metaphorically) for some powerful people.

Pressures ▶ p. 59

How can the need to keep important people (advertisers, politicians or the owners) happy affect the content of newspapers or magazines and television programmes? Read a local German newspaper very carefully, looking out for anything suspicious.
How are local businesses covered?
Is one political party favoured at the expense of the others? Is there a clear distinction between editorial and advertising material? What about minorities?

Politicians are rarely attacked in German newspapers, at least, not along personal lines. You don't see a negative car test printed next to the local dealer's advertisement. Relative prominence and amount of coverage will help learners to decide on the political affiliation of the newspapers they look at.

Teil III

Klausurbeispiele

'They might be spitting in the cannelloni. This is what happens!'

William Leith

We're in a restaurant in a hotel, spending a romantic weekend together. I'm on my best behaviour, having not at all been on my best behaviour in the previous few weeks and months. I am smiling a lot, possibly too much. My girlfriend orders the halibut. Smiling, I also order the halibut. I am making an effort not to be in the least argumentative. I've quibbled too much to this relationship, I know I have; it gives the impression, in small ways, that I am disloyal and unsupportive. This evening, I will not quibble. I will all but simper.

We sip wine. Things are going well. My girlfriend tells me that she hates the lighting in the restaurant. I don't like it either. We both agree that the atmosphere of the restaurant is terribly strained: the combination of the lighting, and the general layout, and the soft, plinking music, makes each table feel strangely exposed. She says: 'I hope you don't think I'm being overcritical.'

'Oh, no. No!'

'I bet you think I'm silly to mention it at all.'

I say, truthfully: 'Not at all. I agree absolutely.'

The music plinks on. My girlfriend thinks it is by Richard Clayderman, and we have one of those short, frowning conversations about Richard Clayderman. I sip wine. We decide to transfer our wine from the glasses into which it has been poured to some slightly nicer glasses intended for water. We smile; this mild act of rebellion is a moment of bonding.

The waiter arrives, holding our halibut, and places it, without much fuss, on our table. It looks normal, if a little flat. It has been grilled, and lies in a little pool of sauce. The vegetables arrive. I put salt and pepper on my halibut, and eat a forkful. My girlfriend eats a forkful. She says: 'I don't think this is cooked properly.'

'Oh ... no. Are you sure?'

'Of course I'm sure.'

I put some more fish into my mouth. My girlfriend is frowning. She says: 'This is definitely not cooked properly. Is yours cooked properly?'

'I'm ... not sure.'

'Well, I can't eat mine.'

I carry on eating. I am being noncommittal. Tension builds. My girlfriend says: 'I'm not eating any more of this.'

'Why don't you complain?'

'Will you taste it and tell me what you think?' she says.

I can see a way forward. I will taste the fish, call the waiter, and send the fish back. Then we will order something else. It is, I believe, the right thing, the supportive thing, to do. She passes her plate across the table. The fish is not quite firm, not quite hot – rather like mine. I eat more of it.

'It's not cooked, is it?'

'I'm not sure.'

'It's like jelly on one side.'

I can, on reflection, see what she means: there does seem to be a jelly-like texture here. Perhaps the fish is uncooked, or undercooked. I can see that this might be the case. I hail the waiter. 'I'm really sorry,' I say, 'and I don't want to cause a fuss, but this is ... not cooked properly. Can we have the vegetarian cannelloni instead?'

The waiter takes the plate away. We sit at our exposed table, which feels like a stage, and wait. Heads turn towards us. My girlfriend sits quietly, her evening, it seems to me, on the edge of ruin. The kitchen door opens, and a man in a chef's costume walks briskly out. He comes to our table and squats by the side of it.

'Who said the fish wasn't cooked?'

We are both silent. My girlfriend hangs her head slightly. I say: 'Uh, her fish, you see ...'

The chef says: 'The fish was not uncooked. I'm passionate about my cooking, and that

is something I just would not do. It would just never happen.'
My girlfriend's head is still hanging. I say: 'Well, her fish had a sort of ... jelly-like texture at the edge.'
'It's supposed to have jelly on it, where it joins the skin.'
'But I think ... there may have been jelly on the underside, too.'
We look at each other. 'I'm sorry,' says the chef, 'but it was not undercooked. I just want to say that.' He walks away. I have a sense of rotating heads in the room.
My girlfriend says: 'Oh my God, they might be spitting in the cannelloni! This is what happens!'
'No. He was cool about it. I could tell.'
'What if somebody spits in it?'
We are silent for a while. I say: 'Nice wine.'
There is more silence. A waiter comes out of the kitchen with a more expensive bottle of wine than the ones on the menu.
'Compliments of the house.' he says.
The cannelloni, when it arrives, tastes of pure phlegm. But this, I am sure, is just imagination.

(The Observer Review, December 7, 1997; The Observer ©)

Assignments

1. What happens to the idea of spending a romantic weekend together?
2. Have a close look at ll. 1–51. Examine the stylistic means used to describe the author's intention of making it a pleasant weekend.
3. Examine the scene in which the chef confronts the journalist and his girl friend. How is the conflict reflected in the use of language?
4. Increasingly journalists seem to make use of personal experiences as the basis for their articles. Do you think this trend towards what has been called "confessional journalism" represents a positive development?
5. Imagine you are the chef and have been invited to write a short column in *The Observer*. You want to use this incident as a basis for your article. Make sure you
   - explain the attitude towards cooking as a profession
   - present the confrontation in the restaurant
   - write about the chef's possible reaction when he is back in the kitchen.

Solutions

1. The chances of the author and his girlfriend spending a romantic week-end together become gradually more and more remote as the meal/the scene proceeds.
At first they get on well. They agree that they don't like the lighting or the music, and "conspire" together to transfer their wine to different glasses. They see this as a small act of rebellion against what we gather is a rather upmarket restaurant where they feel the atmosphere is strained.
However, when the fish comes, the girlfriend says that hers is not properly cooked, and persuades the author to complain. Being very English, he does not want to do so, but decides that he ought to, and asks for cannelloni instead. Both partners find the situation embarrassing, and feel that other diners are watching them. The chef comes to their table and claims that the fish *was* properly cooked, which only makes the couple feel even worse. The girlfriend thinks

that the kitchen staff may spit in the cannelloni as an act of revenge. Although they are given a more expensive bottle of wine as compensation, the meal, and probably the weekend, are ruined.

2. In lines 1–51 the author's style and choice of words indicate that he is trying to get the following concepts across to the reader:
   - the author knows he has been behaving badly, and is making a real effort to do better, e.g. *on my best behaviour, smiling a lot, making an effort not to be... argumentative, disloyal and unsupportive.*
   - the couple are trying to find things to agree on, e.g. the lighting, the atmosphere, the music and the identity of the musician, the sense of being exposed.
   - the couple see themselves as united against the restaurant, e.g. by agreeing that they dislike the features referred to above, and by "rebelliously" pouring their wine into the "wrong" glasses.

3. The chef makes it absolutely clear that he has no doubt whatever about the quality of his cooking in general, and about the fact that the piece of fish in question was properly cooked. He uses emphatic expressions such as *passionate about my cooking, something I just would not do, it would just never happen*. This makes it very difficult to argue with him, because criticism is likely to be taken personally, and there seems to be no room for doubt about the matter. The chef is the professional, and we tend to think twice before we disagree with professionals. (It would be worth adding that a well-known chef enjoys a great deal of prestige in the modern world.) The author has to speak on behalf of his girlfriend, who is clearly intimidated by the chef. The author is also intimidated, and in contrast to the chef, he is afraid to put his case clearly, and uses vague expressions such as, *uh, you see, sort of, jelly-like, I think ...* However, the couple win their case to the extent that they receive a free bottle of wine and an alternative meal. In fact, the restaurant has no alternative in a case like this. The only problem is that the couple are afraid the cannelloni will have been tampered with, so they can't enjoy it.

4. Points which could be made **for** confessional journalism:
   - often interesting/revealing/well-written
   - readers often turn first to this kind of article – compelling reading
   - may help readers to deal with their own problems
   - makes a change from politics etc.

   Points **against**:
   - family and friends of the author may not like the way they are depicted
   - unhealthily self-centred/narcissistic
   - likely to become boring in the long run
   - writers usually people with problems themselves.

5. The introduction should make it clear that a good cook is dedicated to his profession, regards good food/cooking/eating out as one of the most important aspects of life, and takes pride in his work. He (most well-known cooks are men!) firmly believes that everything which comes into his kitchen is of the highest quality and everything which leaves it is perfectly cooked. He also believes that he is more likely to know if food has been prepared properly than his customers.

The confrontation described in the article will have annoyed him and upset him. He takes a very firm line, but may not be quite as convinced that everything is in order as his manner suggests. Claiming that the fish was properly cooked is second nature to him – a defence mechanism. Whether he will be prepared to admit that he could have been in the wrong will be something for the student to decide. The conventions make it essential that the customers are given an alternative meal (plus some kind of present as a rule), whether they are in the right or not.

Possible reactions when he is back in the kitchen:
- perhaps one of his staff cooked the fish and didn't do it properly. In this case the junior cook will be in for a severe telling-off/reprimand.
- Perhaps the customers simply don't know what properly-cooked halibut should be like, in which case the chef will probably let off steam about having to cook for people who don't appreciate fine cooking – and maybe someone did spit in the cannelloni, although this is unlikely to feature in the article. William Leith will have read about legendary acts of revenge of this kind. A chef would almost certainly see things differently.
- The chef may have made a mistake himself. This would be the hardest thing to admit in an article, but in view of the fashion for confessional journalism, perhaps he would be prepared to at least give the customers the benefit of the doubt. However, such a confession could threaten his reputation, and people who go to fashionable restaurants are notoriously fickle. They might go elsewhere next time.

Klausur 2

A Touch of Class

John Cleese and Connie Booth

SYBIL: *(popping her head round the door)* Someone at reception, dear. *(she vanishes)*

    (Basil hurries bad-temperedly into the lobby. Melbury is standing there.)

BASIL: Yes, yes, well, yes?
MELBURY: ... Er, well I was wondering if you could offer me accommodation for a few nights?
BASIL: *(very cross)* Well, have you booked?
MELBURY: ... I'm sorry?
BASIL: Have you booked, have you booked?
MELBURY: No.
BASIL: *(to himself)* Oh dear!
MELBURY: Why, are you full?

BASIL: Oh, we're not full ... we're not full ... of course we're not full!!
MELBURY: I'd like, er ...
BASIL: One moment, one moment, please ... yes?
MELBURY: A single room with a ...
BASIL: Your name, please, could I have your name?
MELBURY: Melbury.

The phone rings; Basil picks it up.

BASIL: *(to Melbury)* One second please. *(to phone)* Hello? ... Ah, yes, Mr O'Reilly, well it's perfectly simple. When I asked you to build me a wall I was rather hoping that instead of just dumping the bricks in a pile you might have found time to cement them together ... you know, one on top of another, in the traditional fashion. *(to Melbury, testily)* Could you fill it in, please? *(to phone)* Oh, splendid! Ah, yes, but when, Mr O'Reilly? *(to Melbury, who is having difficulty with the register)* there – there!! *(to phone)* Yes, but when? Yes, yes, ... ah! ... the flu! *(to Melbury)* Both names, please. *(to phone)* Yes, I should have guessed, Mr O'Reilly, that and the potato famine I suppose ...
MELBURY: I beg your pardon?
BASIL: Would you put both your names, please? ... *(to phone)* Well, will you give me a date?
MELBURY: Er ... I only use one.
BASIL: *(with a withering look)* You don't have a first name?
MELBURY: No, I am Lord Melbury, so I simply sign myself 'Melbury'.

There is a long, long pause.

BASIL: *(to phone)* Go away. *(puts phone down)* ... I'm so sorry to have kept you waiting, your lordship ... I do apologize, please forgive me. Now, was there something, is there something, anything, I can do for you? Anything at all?
MELBURY: Well, I have filled this in ...
BASIL: Oh, please don't bother with that. *(he takes the form and throws it away)* Now, a special room? ... a single? A double? A suite? ... Well, we don't have any suites, but we do have some beautiful doubles with a view ...
MELBURY: No, no, just a single.
BASIL: Just a single! Absolutely! How very wise if I may say so, your honour.
MELBURY: With a bath.
BASIL: Naturally, naturally! *Naturellement! (he roars with laughter)*
MELBURY: I shall be staying for one or two nights ...
BASIL: Oh please! Please ... Manuel!! *(he bangs the bell; nothing happens)* ... Well, it's ... it's rather grey today, isn't it?
MELBURY: Oh, yes, it is, rather.
BASIL: Of course usually down here it's quite beautiful, but today is a real old ... er ... rotter. *(another bang on the bell)* Manuel!!!... Still ... it's good for the wheat.
MELBURY: Yes, er, I suppose so.

(The Complete Fawlty Towers, London: Methuen 1989, pp. 11-12)

Assignments

1. Describe the way in which Basil treats Melbury.
2. Analyse the language used by Basil when he is on the phone to O'Reilly. What do you notice?
3. Basil's behaviour changes completely and abruptly the moment Melbury introduces himself as a Lord. How is this change reflected in the language?
4. A TV-programme guide pointed out that Basil Fawlty is the living image of narrow-mindedness and bad behaviour. Comment on this statement in the light of your knowledge of his character.
5. Imagine you are a guest in the hotel and have witnessed this conversation. You keep a diary in which you write down your views of daily events. What would your entry be for this day?

Solutions

1. At first Basil treats Melbury in a rude, offhand way, repeats instructions to him, and sarcastically says that of course the hotel isn't full, meaning that it is, or that the question was a stupid one (Fawlty Towers unlikely to be popular with visitors to the area). He treats a phone-call to Mr O'Reilly the builder as more important than dealing with Melbury, and becomes very impatient when it appears that Melbury only has one name.
   As soon as Basil realises that he is dealing with a Lord (or thinks he is – in fact Melbury is an impostor and confidence trickster), his manner becomes ultra-respectful, subservient, crawling. Everything in the hotel is at Melbury's disposal. Basil is nervous at having such a distinguished guest on the premises, so he laughs loudly, tries out his French and his small-talk, and makes a big thing of summoning Manuel, the Spanish waiter.

2. When Basil talks to Mr O'Reilly he treats him almost as if he is a child, who needs even the most basic things explaining to him, including O'Reilly's own job as a builder, e.g. *you know, one on top of the other, in the traditional fashion.* The tone is also ironic/sarcastic, e.g *I was rather hoping ....* which implies that it is almost too much to expect O'Reilly actually to do the job he was asked to do. The later part of the monologue makes it clear that Basil is all too well aware of the way O'Reilly makes excuses for not finishing jobs on time. When O'Reilly mentions the flu, Basil replies *Yes, I should have guessed*, and adds another, totally unbelievable excuse of his own ... *the potato famine, I suppose.*

3. Language before Melbury introduces himself as a Lord:
   - impatient, using repetition, e.g. *Yes, yes, well, yes? Have you booked, have you booked?*
   - sarcastic, e.g. *of course we're not full*
   - breaking normal rules of discourse, particularly in a hotel situation, by interrupting a guest, using emphatic language, e.g. *Your **name** please, could I have your name?*

   After Melbury introduces himself:
   - use of emphatic language for extreme politeness, e.g. *I'm **so** sorry, I **do** apologize, **please** forgive me.*

- exaggerated subservience, e.g. *is there something, anything I can do for you.*
- Basil agrees with everything the guest says, e.g. *Just a single! Absolutely! How very **wise** if I may say so.*
- feels the need to make small-talk, however banal the topics e.g. the weather and the farming prospects, which neither of them is likely to be the slightest bit interested in.

4. (Students can also make use of what they know about Basil Fawlty from the extract in the student's book.)
   narrow-mindedness:
   - very negative attitude to Mr Johnson – assumes he cannot be intelligent because of the way he dresses and speaks – thinks of him as little better than an orang-utang.
   - Basil is a mass of prejudices of all kinds – unfavourable (Irish people, people like Mr Johnson, and favourable (see next item)
   - believes in class distinction – unthinking respect for doctors and aristocrats whatever their character
   - believes in a formal dress code.
   - very traditional and old-fashioned – references to older British heroes/ role models, attitude to the aristocracy etc.

   bad behaviour:
   - rude to customers who are not of the "approved type"
   - impatient
   - sarcastic
   - shouts at people, uses emphatic language inappropriately
   - behaves in a childish way (e.g. the monkey imitation) in the presence of customers.

5. Watched the manager of the hotel in action this afternoon. Seems to be a very strange type. At first he was very rude to this customer who came in, shouted at him, said he should have booked, pretended the hotel was full. Then right in the middle of talking to him he took a phone call – seemed to be about problems with a builder. Surely he could have asked the man to ring back. Then there was some fuss about the visitor's name. Apparently he'd only put one name down on the form, and Fawlty wanted two. It then emerged that the man only used one name because he was a Lord!
   At this point there was a long pause while Fawlty took in the news. Then he switched to being the ultra-perfect host – he really crawled to the man – totally overdid it. Would have given the man a suite if they'd had one. Agreed with everything he said, used a bit of French, shouted dramatically for Manuel – he must be the porter – then tried to chat to the noble guest – without much success. At one point he roared with laughter for no good reason. Under the surface I would say he's extremely nervous, even hysterical. I really don't know what to make of him.